STUDENT UNIT G

UNIT

OCR(A) AS F964

History

The USA and the Cold War in Asia
1945–75 (Option B5)

Derrick Murphy

Philip Allan Updates, an imprint of Hodder Education, an Hachette UK company, Market Place, Deddington, Oxfordshire OX15 0SE

Orders

Bookpoint Ltd, 130 Milton Park, Abingdon, Oxfordshire OX14 4SB
tel: 01235 827720
fax: 01235 400454
e-mail: uk.orders@bookpoint.co.uk
Lines are open 9.00 a.m.–5.00 p.m., Monday to Saturday, with a 24-hour message answering service. You can also order through the Philip Allan Updates website: www.philipallan.co.uk

© Philip Allan Updates 2009

ISBN 978-0-340-99040-7

First printed 2009
Impression number 5 4 3 2 1
Year 2014 2013 2012 2011 2010 2009

This guide has been written specifically to support students preparing for the OCR Specification A AS History Unit F964 examination. The content has been neither approved nor endorsed by OCR and remains the sole responsibility of the author.

Typeset by DC Graphic Design, Swanley Village, Kent
Printed by MPG Books, Bodmin

Hachette UK's policy is to use papers that are natural, renewable and recyclable products and made from wood grown in sustainable forests. The logging and manufacturing processes are expected to conform to the environmental regulations of the country of origin.

Contents

Introduction

■ ■ ■

Content Guidance

■ ■ ■

Questions and Answers

Introduction

Aims of the unit

Unit F964 is worth 25% of the A-level course or 50% of the AS. The subject of Study Topic 5 is: *The USA and the Cold War in Asia 1945–75.* This is a document studies unit.

According to the OCR specification:

> *This option examines the basis of US involvement in Asia after 1945 and the changing nature of its policy to contain communism in China, Korea and Vietnam. Candidates will need to understand why this failed in some areas (China and Vietnam) yet had more success in others (Japan and South Korea). With Vietnam, the focus is on the relative importance of the reasons for a growing US involvement, from Truman to Nixon, and the problems of failure and disengagement. A detailed knowledge of Chinese and Soviet policy is **not** required except insofar as they affected US policy during this period.*

There are no prescribed documents for you to study. Instead you will be presented with information that is 'unseen'. Normally there will be either four or five sources. Their maximum combined length will be 500 words. Where five sources are used it will be normal practice for four of these sources to be 'primary' documents. Most sources used in questions will be written, but on occasion either pictorial or numerical sources may be used where appropriate. Although the sources used are 'unseen', you will be expected to have a knowledge of the topic to which the sources refer. You will therefore be expected to place the sources 'in context' and may well be asked to comment on their utility and reliability.

You will need knowledge of the topic and the ability to explain historical events, as well as to analyse and assess source material. Questions require you to provide clear information that directly answers the question. In addition, in sub-question (b), examiners are looking for detailed and precise supporting own knowledge to demonstrate that your statements are accurate. These examples need to be linked clearly to your argument.

The USA and the Cold War in Asia, 1945–75 is Study Topic 5 of Unit F964 European and World History Enquiries, Option B Modern: 1774–1975. You need to be prepared to answer two sub-questions on a specific topic within the course. Sub-question (a) requires you to compare information contained in two sources. Sub-question (b) requires you to use information from all the sources, and your own knowledge, to answer an analytical-style question. Tables 1 and 2 are marking grids for the two sub-questions. This book deals exclusively with *The USA and the Cold War in Asia, 1945–75.*

Table 1 Marking grid for sub-question (a)

AOs	AO1a	AO1b	AO2a
Total for each question = 30	Recall, select and deploy historical knowledge appropriately, and communicate knowledge and understanding of history in a clear and effective manner	Demonstrate understanding of the past through explanation, analysis and arriving at substantiated judgements of: – key concepts such as causation, consequence, continuity, change and significance within a historical context – the relationships between key features and characteristics of the periods studied	As part of a historical enquiry, analyse and evaluate a range of appropriate source material with discrimination
Level IA	• Accurate use of a range of appropriate historical terminology • Answer is clearly structured and coherent, communicates accurately and legibly **6**	• Answer is consistently and relevantly analytical, with developed comparison and judgement • Clear and accurate understanding of key concepts relevant to analysis and to the topic • Clear and accurate understanding of the significance of issues in their historical context **8**	• Response provides a focused comparison and/or contrast of both content and provenance • Evaluates qualities such as reliability, completeness, consistency, typicality, and especially utility, in relation to the question **16**
Level IB	• Accurate use of a range of appropriate historical terminology • Answer is clearly structured and coherent, communicates accurately and legibly **6**	• Judgements are supported by appropriate references to both content and provenance • Very good level of understanding of key concepts • Clear and accurate understanding of the significance of issues in their historical context **7**	• Response provides an effective comparison and/or contrast of both content and provenance • Evaluates a range of qualities of authenticity, completeness, consistency, typicality and usefulness in relation to the question **13–15**

AOs	AO1a	AO1b	AO2a
Level II	• Generally accurate use of historical terminology • Answer is structured and mostly coherent, writing is legible and communication is generally clear 5	• Good attempt at explanation/analysis but uneven overall judgements • Mostly clear and accurate understanding of key concepts • Clear understanding of the significance of most relevant issues in their historical context 6	• Provides a relevant comparison and/or contrast of both content and provenance • Answer lacks completeness in evaluating most of the range of available criteria (e.g. limited use of the introductions and/or attributions) 11–12
Level III	• Answer includes relevant historical terminology but this may not be extensive or always accurately used • Most of the answer is organised and structured; the answer is mostly legible and clearly communicated 4	• A mixture of internal analysis and discussion of similarities and/or differences. A judgement is unlikely • Some/uneven understanding of many key concepts relevant to analysis and of many concepts relevant to the topic • Uneven understanding of the significance of most relevant issues in their historical context 5	• Provides a comparison and/or contrast • Makes limited links with the sources by focusing too much on content or on provenance • Uneven organisation, confining the comparison to the second half of the answer or simply to a concluding paragraph 9–10
Level IV	• There may be some evidence that is tangential or irrelevant • Some unclear and/or underdeveloped and/or disorganised sections; mostly satisfactory level of communication 3	• Mostly satisfactory understanding of key concepts • Mostly satisfactory explanation, but some unlinked though relevant assertions, description/narrative • There is no judgement 4	• Response attempts a comparison and/or contrast but the comment is largely sequential • Few points of comparative provenance or discussion of similarity/difference of content 7–8

AOs	AO1a	AO1b	AO2a
Level V	• There may be inaccuracies and irrelevant material • Some accurate use of relevant historical terminology but often inaccurate/ inappropriate use • Often unclear and disorganised sections; writing is often clear if basic, but there may be some illegibility and weak prose where the sense is not clear **2**	• General and sometimes inaccurate understanding of key concepts relevant to analysis and of concepts relevant to the topic • General or weak understanding of the significance of most relevant issues in their historical context **3**	• Identifies some points of agreement and/or disagreement • The comparison and/or contrast is implicit • There is no judgement **5–6**
Level VI	• Much irrelevance and inaccuracy • Answer may have little organisation or structure; weak use of English and poor organisation **1**	• Limited explanation but mainly description/ narrative • Very little understanding of key concepts **2**	• Very weak commentary on one point of agreement/ disagreement • Sources may be paraphrased with no real attempt to compare and/or contrast **3–4**
Level VII	• No understanding of the topic or of the question's requirements • Totally irrelevant answer • Very poor use of English **0**	• Weak explanation, and descriptive/narrative commentary on the sources • No understanding of key concepts **0–1**	• No attempt to provide a comparison and/or contrast • Sources are paraphrased or copied out **0–2**

Table 2 Marking grid for sub-question (b)

AOs	AO1a	AO1b	AO2a	AO2b
Total mark for the question = 70	Recall, select and deploy historical knowledge appropriately, and communicate knowledge and understanding of history in a clear and effective manner	Demonstrate understanding of the past through explanation, analysis and arriving at substantiated judgements of: – key concepts such as causation, consequence, continuity, change and significance within a historical context – the relationships between key features and characteristics of the periods studied	As part of a historical enquiry, analyse and evaluate a range of appropriate source material with discrimination	Analyse and evaluate, in relation to the historical context, how aspects of the past have been interpreted and represented in different ways
Level IA	• Uses a wide range of accurate, detailed and relevant evidence • Accurate and confident use of appropriate historical terminology • Answer is clearly structured and coherent, communicates accurately and legibly **9–10**	• Clear and accurate understanding of key concepts relevant to analysis and to the topic • Clear and accurate understanding of the significance of issues in their historical context • Answer is consistently and relevantly analytical, with developed explanations leading to careful judgements **11–12**	• Excellent analysis and evaluation of all sources, with high levels of discrimination. • Analyses and evaluates the limitations of the sources and what is required to add to their completeness as a set **26–28**	• Excellent analysis and evaluation of the historical interpretation, using all sources and own knowledge to reach a clear conclusion • Fully understands that the sources may either support or refute the interpretation **20**

AOs	AO1a	AO1b	AO2a	AO2b
Level IB	• Uses accurate, detailed and relevant evidence • Accurate use of a range of appropriate historical terminology • Answer is clearly structured and mostly coherent, written accurately and legibly 8	• Clear and accurate understanding of most key concepts relevant to analysis and to the topic • Clear understanding of the significance of issues in their historical context • Judgements are supported by appropriate references to both content and provenance 9–10	• Focused analysis and evaluation of all sources, with high levels of discrimination • Analyses and evaluates the limitations of the sources and what is required to add to their completeness as a set 23–25	• Focused analysis and evaluation of the historical interpretation, using all sources and own knowledge to reach a clear conclusion • Understands that the sources may either support or refute the interpretation 17–19
Level II	• Uses mostly accurate, detailed and relevant evidence which demonstrates a competent command of the topic • Generally accurate use of historical terminology • Answer is structured and mostly coherent, writing is legible and communication is generally clear 7	• Mostly clear and accurate understanding of key concepts • Clear understanding of the significance of most relevant issues in their historical context • Good attempt at explanation/analysis but uneven overall judgements 8	• Focused analysis and evaluation of most of the sources, with good levels of discrimination • Analyses and evaluates some of the limitations of the sources and what is required to add to their completeness as a set 20–22	• Focused analysis and evaluation of the historical interpretation, using most of the sources and appropriate own knowledge to reach a clear conclusion • There may be some imbalance between discussion of the sources and use of external knowledge in evaluating the interpretation 14–16

AOs	AO1a	AO1b	AO2a	AO2b
Level III	• Uses accurate and relevant evidence, which demonstrates some command of the topic, but there may be some inaccuracy • Answer includes relevant historical terminology but this may not be extensive or always accurately used • Most of the answer is organised and structured; the answer is mostly legible and clearly communicated 6	• Shows a sound understanding of key concepts • Sound awareness of the significance of issues in their historical context • Attempts an explanation/ analysis but overall judgement may be incomplete 6–7	• Refers to most of the sources to illustrate an argument rather than analysing and evaluating their evidence • Aware of some of the sources' limitations either individually or as a set 17–19	• Sound analysis and evaluation of the historical interpretation • There may be some description and unevenness between use of own knowledge and use of sources • Answers that use the sources but no own knowledge in assessing the interpretation have a Level III ceiling 11–13
Level IV	• There is deployment of relevant knowledge but level/accuracy of detail will vary; there may be some evidence that is tangential or irrelevant • Some unclear and/or underdeveloped and/or disorganised sections; mostly satisfactory level of communication 4–5	• Mostly satisfactory understanding of key concepts • Some explanation, but not always linked to the question • Assertions, description/ narrative will characterise part of the answer 4–5	• Sources are discussed sequentially • Considers some of the limitations of the sources, but may not establish a sense of different views 14–16	• Some analysis and evaluation of the historical interpretation, with increasing amounts of description • Response is more unbalanced than Level III in using sources and own knowledge • Answers that use own knowledge but make no use of the sources in assessing the interpretation have a Level IV ceiling 8–10

AOs	AO1a	AO1b	AO2a	AO2b
Level V	• Some relevant historical knowledge is deployed: this may be generalised and patchy. There may be inaccuracies and irrelevant material • Some accurate use of relevant historical terminology but often inaccurate/ inappropriate use • Often unclear and disorganised sections; writing will often be basic and there may be some illegibility and weak prose where the sense is not clear **3**	• General and sometimes inaccurate understanding of key concepts relevant to analysis and of concepts relevant to the topic • General or weak understanding of the significance of most relevant issues in their historical context **3**	• Limited attempt to use the sources or discriminate between them; they are discussed sequentially • Sources will be used for reference and illustration of an argument **11–13**	• Mainly description, with limited comment on the context of the question • Little effective analysis of how far the sources support the interpretation **6–7**
Level VI	• Limited use of relevant evidence; much irrelevance and inaccuracy • Little organisation or structure • Weak use of English and poor organisation **2**	• Very little understanding of key concepts • No explanation • Assertion, description/ narrative predominate **2**	• Weak application of the sources to the question • Weak attempt at analysis **5–10**	• Weak contextual knowledge • Mainly description, with weak evaluation of the historical interpretation **3–5**
Level VII	• No understanding of the topic or of the question's requirements; little relevant and accurate knowledge • Very fragmentary and disorganised response; very poor use of English and some incoherence **0–1**	• No understanding of key concepts • Weak explanation, assertion, description/ narrative **0–1**	• Very weak application of the sources to the question • No attempt at analysis **0–4**	• Very weak attempt at evaluating the historical interpretation • Heavily descriptive • No contextual knowledge **0–2**

The examination paper

The examination paper concentrates on one major topic within the specification. In F964 Option B there are five study topics. You will be expected to answer sub-questions on only one of these topics. In this case both sub-questions will be on Topic 5, *The USA and the Cold War in Asia, 1945–75*, which is the final study topic on the examination paper. You are required to answer two sub-questions. The examination paper lasts 1 hour 30 minutes. In that time you will be expected to answer two sub-questions. One is worth 30 marks and the other is worth 70 marks. You should therefore apportion your time accordingly. You should spend approximately 30 minutes answering sub-question (a) and 1 hour answering sub-question (b).

The format of the sub-questions in a typical examination paper is as follows:

Unit F964 – European and World History Enquiries: Option B Modern: 1774–1975

Answer both sub-questions from Study Topic 5: The USA and the Cold War in Asia, 1945–75

(a) Study two sources which are identified in the examination paper.

Compare the information presented in these sources concerning the specific course topic mentioned in the question. **(Total: 30 marks)**

(b) Study all the sources.

Use your own knowledge to assess how far the sources support a specific interpretation contained within the topic identified for discussion and analysis. **(Total: 70 marks)**

Examinable skills

A total of 100 marks are available for Unit F964. Marks will be awarded for demonstrating the following skills:
- Analysing and evaluating sources.
- Remembering, choosing and using historical knowledge to support analysis of sources.
- Analysing, explaining and reaching a judgement.
- Showing links between the key factors of your explanation.

Focusing on the requirements of the sub-questions

Read the sub-questions carefully. Then study the sources relevant to the sub-question.

Sub-question (a) requires a comparison of historical evidence in two sources. Also consider the attribution of the two sources. When were they written? Who wrote them? What was the motive in producing the source?

Sub-question (b) requires you to study all the sources and use your own knowledge to address an analytical question. You will be required to integrate your own knowledge with information from the sources to produce a balanced (for and against) argument which reaches a judgement.

Remembering, choosing and using historical knowledge
In sub-question (b), when you have established what the question requires, you must decide which aspects of your own knowledge are relevant. Examiners are looking for an answer that covers the use of all the sources and relevant use of your own knowledge. You must then arrange this information in a logical order to create a plan for your answer.

Once your structure is in place, you must develop it using specific examples. Try to ensure that your examples are detailed. You should include relevant dates; names of people, places, institutions and events, statistics and appropriate technical vocabulary. Examiners will reward both range and depth of knowledge.

Analysing, explaining and reaching a judgement
Merely describing the content of a source or telling the story of an event will not score well. It is expected that your answer will be arranged analytically, addressing different aspects of the answer in turn. In sub-question (a), if you are asked to compare information between two sources the first part of your answer will identify comparisons and the second part of your answer will deal with contrasts within and between the sources. The final part of your answer will be a statement which reaches a judgement.

In sub-question (b) it is useful to divide the sources into those which support one side of the argument and those which deal with the other. Ensure that you integrate relevant own knowledge with source evidence. It is good practice to make these links at the end of each paragraph. It is also important that your answers reach a clear judgement.

Showing links between the key factors of your explanation
In order to achieve the highest marks, you must highlight links between the factors that you have selected. This could mean demonstrating the relative importance of the different factors, or showing how the factors were dependent on each other.

How to use this guide

First, make sure that you understand the layout of the examination paper, the pattern of the marks and the types of question asked, all of which are explained above. Study the outline of the content required, which is given in the Content Guidance section. Try to:

- master the vocabulary and concepts given there
- establish clearly the important individuals and institutions which shaped the events of these years
- assess the extent of change in US policy between 1945 and 1975

The most important part of the guide is the Questions and Answers section, which provides two examples of the kinds of question that you will be asked. It is important to work through these, studying the two sets of sample answers provided and the examiner's comments. The first answer to each question is an A-grade response which, although not perfect, gives a good idea of what is required. The purpose of the second (C-grade) answer is to illustrate some of the common errors made by students.

Content
Guidance

The specification for this part of Unit F964 Option B is divided into four key issues:

- How successfully did the USA seek to contain communism in Asia to 1950?
- How far did the Korean War and its origins (1950–53) change the USA's conduct of the Cold War in Asia?
- Why and with what results did the USA become involved in Vietnam to 1968?
- Why did the USA fail to win the Vietnam War?

The main focus is on the development of US policy in Asia from 1945, with specific emphasis on the US attempts to contain communism in China, Korea and Vietnam. You need to know the role of the USA in 1945 and how its policies developed towards Japan, China, Korea and southeast Asia. You will be expected to explain why some US policies, such as those towards Japan and Korea, were more successful than those towards China and southeast Asia. To help you understand what will be required for this AS unit, the content has been broken down into sections. Where appropriate, the section ends with an extended explanation of key terms and personalities.

ntroductory survey

The USA and Asia, 1945–75

On 6 and 9 August 1945, US B-29 bombers based on the Pacific island of Tinian dropped atomic bombs on the Japanese cities of Hiroshima and Nagasaki. These attacks brought to an end the Second World War in Asia. On 2 September, on the decks of the USS *Missouri*, in Tokyo Bay, representatives of Japan signed the surrender document. The event marked the end of a conflict which had raged in Asia continuously since the Japanese invasion of China in 1937. It also confirmed the USA as the dominant military power in east Asia.

From 1945 the USA played a central role in the affairs of east Asia.

The period 1945–75 in Asia was characterised by two major historical events. The first was the decolonisation of much of the region by European powers. In the period 1945–57 European states withdrew from the countries known today as India, Pakistan, Bangladesh, Sri Lanka, Myanmar, Malaysia, Laos, Vietnam, Cambodia and Indonesia. In addition, the USA gave independence to the Philippines. In some cases political power was handed over peacefully, as in the Indian sub-continent. However, in other areas such as French Indo-China, European rule only came to an end after a protracted war for independence.

The other major event was the extension of the Cold War to Asia. Beginning in Europe at the end of the Second World War, the Cold War spread to Asia through the Communist victory in the Chinese Civil War of 1946–49 and the Korean War of 1950–53. The conflict between Communist and non-Communist forces affected the process of European decolonisation. Conflicts related to decolonisation in Indonesia, French Indo-China and Malaya all involved Communist insurgents attempting to create a Communist post-colonial government.

In the middle of this process the USA became a major participant.

The USA saw itself as the defender of the Free World against the expansion of communism, first in Europe, then in Asia. To the USA the Iron Curtain in Europe had been joined by the Bamboo Curtain in Asia. In its attempt to prevent the spread of communism the USA became involved in defending colonial regimes against Communist liberation movements. The USA began to believe in the 'domino effect': if one country fell to a Communist regime, it would only be a matter of time before a neighbouring country fell. This helps to explain why the USA became involved in France's war in Indo-China, 1946–54, and eventually in its own war in Laos, Vietnam and Cambodia.

Its strategy of resisting the spread of communism drew the USA into two major conflicts. From 1950 to 1953 it was the major participant in the UN forces that fought North Korea and the Chinese People's Volunteer Army in the Korean War. From March

1965 US ground troops were deployed in the conflict in South Vietnam, a commitment which was to last until January 1973.

The cost of US military commitment ran to billions of dollars and hundreds of thousands of men killed or wounded. The USA lost approximately 35,000 service personnel in the Korean War, and approximately 57,000 were killed in the Vietnam War.

Both conflicts had a profound impact on the domestic politics of the USA.

President Harry Truman (president 1945–53) was heavily criticised for the war in Korea, particularly after the Chinese intervention in late 1950. In particular, Republican Senator **Joseph McCarthy** from Wisconsin complained that Truman was soft on communism and accused his government of harbouring Communists and Communist sympathisers. These attacks help to explain why the Republicans won the 1952 presidential election.

By 1967 opposition to US involvement in Vietnam had begun to grow at home. Anti-war demonstrations became more frequent and an anti-war candidate, Eugene McCarthy (no relation to Joseph McCarthy), stood against Democratic President Lyndon Johnson (known as 'LBJ') in the early primary elections which preceded the presidential election of 1968. The growing opposition to the war and the USA's failure to achieve a clear military victory led Johnson to announce in March 1968 that he would not seek another term as president.

The USA's involvement in Asia from 1945 to 1975 involved enormous military effort and commitment. On one hand, it could be argued that US intervention in the Korean War was a success as it prevented the North Korean acquisition of South Korea. (To this day, a peace treaty has yet to be signed and, technically, North and South Korea are still at war.) In South Vietnam, Laos and Cambodia, US involvement can be seen as a failure. In 1975 North Vietnam invaded and conquered South Vietnam. In the same year the Communist Pathet Lao took control of Laos and the Khmer Rouge took control of Cambodia. The 'domino effect' seemed to have worked in Indo-China.

Key figures

President Harry S. Truman (1884–1972): US president from 1945 to 1953. Truman succeeded Franklin D. Roosevelt in April 1945, shortly before the end of the Second World War. He was president during the early years of the Cold War and in March 1947 he introduced the policy of containing communism. In 1950 he confronted the expansion of communism in Korea. His most controversial decision in the Korean War was to dismiss the UN commander, General Douglas MacArthur, for wishing to extend the war to include attacks on Communist China. From 1950 Truman provided extensive financial and military assistance to the French fighting the Vietminh.

Joseph McCarthy (1908–57): a Republican Senator for the state of Wisconsin from 1947 until his death in 1957. He reached national notoriety from 1950 when he began to allege that Truman's Democratic administration contained Communists and Communist sympathisers. McCarthy complained that US society was permeated with

Communist links. He led 'witch-hunts' against suspected Communists in Hollywood, the media and the government. An important instrument in McCarthy's anti-Communist campaign was the Un-American Activities Committee of the US House of Representatives. McCarthy's accusations helped defeat the Democrats in the 1952 presidential and congressional elections. Once the Republicans had won control of the government, McCarthy's usefulness began to wane. In 1954 he attempted to root out communism in the armed forces. This brought him into conflict with President Eisenhower. From 1954 his influence began to diminish rapidly until his death from alcoholism in 1957.

The USA and Asia, 1945–52

The recovery of Japan, 1945–52

In September 1945 the USA was at the height of its military power in Asia. Japan had been defeated and US General **Douglas MacArthur**, Allied Supreme Commander in Japan, ensured that the USSR would not participate in the country's occupation. In 1945 the USA had the second largest army on earth, after the Soviet Red Army. It had the largest navy and the largest air force. Its strategic air force could attack targets hundreds of miles away with nuclear weapons.

The immediate task facing the USA from 1945 was the reconstruction of Japan, which had been devastated by US air raids. In one air raid on the capital, Tokyo, in the summer of 1945 approximately 200,000 civilians died. In August 1945 a further 160,000 died in two nuclear weapons attacks on Hiroshima and Nagasaki. The US naval blockade had cut Japan off from sources of raw materials and food. With the war ended, the country seemed on the verge of economic collapse. The old political system had been replaced by an Allied administration. The only link with the past was the retention of the emperor, Hirohito, as head of state. However, he was now merely a national figurehead with minimal political power.

The key Allied administrator in Japan from September 1945 was General Douglas MacArthur, who was appointed to take charge of the Supreme Command of the Allied Powers (SCAP). He had the final say in all decisions: an Allied Council did exist, including representatives of Nationalist China, the USSR and the British Commonwealth, but it had only an advisory role. MacArthur had the task of completely rebuilding the political, administrative and economic structure of Japan.

Immediately after the end of the war territorial changes were made to the former Japanese empire. The USSR received South Sakhalin and acquired the Kurile Islands. Nationalist China recovered the island of Formosa, later to be known as Taiwan. Japanese possessions in the Pacific islands were administered by the USA and the British Commonwealth. Finally, the Korean peninsula was temporarily divided into two military zones. North of the 38th parallel (38 degrees north of the equator) the USSR administered the peninsula. South of that line, the USA was the occupying power. The two powers set up rival Korean administrations in what was regarded as a temporary arrangement.

Within Japan MacArthur launched a political revolution. In the years 1945–47 he led the Allied campaign to punish Japanese war criminals. The most senior Japanese politician to be tried and executed was General Tojo, the wartime Japanese prime minister. MacArthur ensured that the emperor would not face a court hearing. In addition, MacArthur dismantled the administrative structure of the Japanese armed forces. In a new constitution, created by SCAP, Japan was to be limited to coastal defence forces and renounced the right to wage war.

In the economic sphere MacArthur attempted to break up the large Japanese business corporations, known as *zaibatsu*, which along with the armed forces had been blamed for Japan's aggressive foreign policy in the 1930s and 1940s. This was part of a plan to transform Japan into a free market capitalist economy along US lines. In the countryside MacArthur broke up large estates and gave land to tenant farmers.

Perhaps the most significant change came in the realm of politics. The new Japanese Constitution of 1947 turned Japan into a constitutional monarchy with a democratically elected government. For the first time in Japanese history women were given the right to vote.

By late 1947 Japan had been transformed. However, inflationary pressure in the economy and the rise of communism led to intervention by SCAP. Measures were introduced to control inflation, while the US government gave preferential treatment to trade with Japan and allowed it to purchase raw materials at a preferential rate. The outbreak of the Korean War in June 1950 brought a huge boost for the Japanese economy, as the country became the major UN supply base for the war.

MacArthur ceased to be head of SCAP at the outbreak of the Korean War, when he was appointed senior commander of the UN forces. In September 1951 the Allied powers formally signed a peace treaty with Japan, the Treaty of San Francisco. The treaty came into force at the end of April 1952.

Under the treaty Japan gave up all rights to Korea, South Sakhalin, the Kurile Islands, Taiwan and its Pacific possessions. The USA was granted a major military base on Okinawa, in the Ryuku Islands, south of the Japanese mainland. This treaty was signed at the height of the Korean War, and the USSR and some of its Communist allies in Eastern Europe refused to sign it.

However, it brought to an end a remarkable chapter in Japanese history. In 6 short years Japan had been transformed from a military dictatorship into a western-style democracy with a capitalist-style economy. Japan had become pivotal to US policy in the far east, as a bastion against the spread of communism, a major US military base and an example of how eastern states could develop along democratic lines.

The fall of China, 1945–49

One of the most significant developments in the immediate postwar history of Asia was the final stages of the Chinese Civil War. From 1927 the armed forces of China's Nationalist Party (known as the **Guomindang**) under Chiang Kai-Shek (Jiang Jieshi) had fought Communist Chinese forces under Mao Zedong.

From 1937 to 1945 a cease-fire was agreed in order to mount a joint defence of China against Japanese invasion. During this Sino-Japanese War, the Nationalists fought the Japanese in southern China and the Communists fought them in northwest China. Throughout the Second World War the Nationalists were supplied by the Allies, mainly the USA. The Nationalists were regarded as the legitimate government of China by the outside world and when the UN Security Council was founded they took China's seat on it.

In 1945 the USA sent General George C. Marshall to secure an extension of the compromise between the Nationalists and the Communists. Unfortunately, in 1946 Chiang Kai-Shek decided to reopen the civil war and attacked Communist areas in north China, in particular in Manchuria, held until 1945 by Japan. In the ensuing conflict Mao's Communists were victorious.

There are many reasons for the Communist victory. They were better led and adopted very effective military tactics under their commander Lin Biao. In contrast, the Nationalists were divided by internal rivalries and suffered from widespread corruption. Although the USA supported the Nationalists with hundreds of millions of dollars in military aid, its main area of interest between 1946 and 1949 was Europe, where it was confronting the USSR in the early stages of the Cold War. In 1947 the USA pledged $13 billion in aid to Europe under the Marshall Plan. In 1948–49 the USA was involved in the Berlin airlift crisis.

The turning point in the Civil War came in 1948, in the Battle of Suchow, north of Shanghai. Communist forces routed the Nationalists and gained control of most of China north of the Yangtse River. In early 1949 the Communists occupied Nanjing, the Nationalist capital, and Chiang Kai-Shek fled to Taiwan. Although no official treaty ended the Civil War, 1949 saw the Communists triumph with the declaration by Mao of the People's Republic of China.

The Communist victory in China transformed the political map of the far east. Communism had now established itself in the world's most populous country. The Communist threat had spread from Europe to Asia and was now a global threat to the USA. Almost as soon as the Communists had won in 1949, recriminations began in the USA. President Truman was accused of losing China. Republican Senator Joseph McCarthy began accusing the Democrat government of being soft on communism and also, most seriously, containing known Communists and Communist sympathisers.

The fall of China to the Communists led to a reappraisal of US policy in the far east. In August 1949 Secretary of State Dean Acheson rebutted claims that the USA had lost China and blamed Nationalist defeat squarely on Chiang Kai-Shek. Then, on

12 January 1950, Acheson made a major policy speech to the National Press Club in the USA. He claimed that Japan, Okinawa and the Philippine Islands were within the US 'defence perimeter' in the far east, stating:

> Our defensive dispositions against Asiatic aggression used to be based on the west coast of the American continent. Now...our line of defence runs through the chain of islands fringing the coast of Asia. It starts from the Philippines and continues through the Ryuku Archipelago, which includes its main bastion, Okinawa. Then it bends back through Japan and the Aleutian Island chain to Alaska.

Unfortunately, Acheson made no direct reference to the Korean peninsula or Taiwan. This placed in question US commitment to defending South Korea and the Nationalist Chinese on Taiwan.

NSC68, April 1950

By 1950 the USA was facing a new phase of the Cold War. In March 1947 President Truman had launched the Truman Doctrine, which sought to contain the spread of communism. The Truman Doctrine was aimed at Europe, but the Communist victory in the Chinese Civil War took the Cold War into a new, global phase. The USA now faced a Communist challenge in Asia. The USSR, Communist China and Communist-administered North Korea posed a new threat. In southeast Asia the Communist-dominated Vietminh forces were fighting the French for control of Vietnam. In Malaya Communist guerrillas were at war with British forces. This was the climate in which on 14 April 1950 the US president received an important new National Security Council (NSC) policy document which went by the name NSC68.

NSC68 set out a possible way forward for US foreign and military policy during the Cold War. The document was the NSC response to President Truman's request that it assess the Communist threat following the Soviet explosion of an atomic bomb in August 1949. According to NSC68:

> The gravest threat to the security of the United States within the foreseeable future stems from the hostile designs and formidable power of the USSR, and from the nature of the Soviet system...The risk of war with the USSR is sufficient to warrant, in common prudence, timely and adequate preparation by the United States.

Meeting this challenge, said NSC68, required the USA to:

> ...develop a level of military readiness which can be maintained as long as necessary as a deterrent to Soviet aggression,...as a source of encouragement to nations resisting Soviet political aggression, and as an adequate basis for immediate military commitments and for rapid mobilization should war prove unavoidable...

It also said the USA must:

> ...strengthen the orientation toward the United States of the non-Soviet nations; and help such of those nations as are able and willing to make an important

contribution to US security, to increase their economic and political stability and their military capability.

This document seemed to be the logical result of the tensions between the USA and the USSR which had been developing into a cold war since 1945. It suggested that the USA faced a global confrontation with international communism. The fall of China to communism in 1949 was merely a part of this process. The creation in 1949 of the North Atlantic Treaty Organisation (NATO), a military alliance to defend Europe, fitted in with this world-view. However, it was also an important departure from previous US policy. Before NSC68 the USA had relied on its monopoly in nuclear weapons to provide adequate national defence. Now that this nuclear monopoly had gone, and the Communist challenge had been extended to Asia, NSC68 called for a massive increase in US military capacity.

NSC68 was merely a policy document recommending a possible new direction for US defence policy. But possibility was turned into reality by events which occurred in Korea in June 1950.

Glossary

Guomindang: the Nationalist Party in China, which ruled much of mainland China from 1927 to 1949 but was defeated by the Communist forces led by Mao Zedong. Note: there are two main systems for transliteration of Chinese characters, Wade-Giles and the more modern *pinyin*. This version of the name is pinyin; according to the Wade Giles system it was spelt Kuomintang.

Key figures

General Douglas MacArthur (1880–1964): the USA's most decorated soldier in the First World War, in the Second World War MacArthur attempted to defend the Philippines against Japanese invasion but was forced to leave. He led the US and Allied armies against Japan in the southwest Pacific. MacArthur accepted the Japanese surrender on board the USS *Missouri* on 2 September 1945. In 1950 he became UN commander in Korea but was controversially dismissed by President Truman in 1951.

The Korean War and its consequences

The origins of the Korean War

Korea is a peninsula located between China and Japan. Although a separate Korean culture and state had existed in the past, much of the modern history of Korea had been associated with political submission to either the Chinese or Japanese empires. Until 1905 Korea had been regarded as part of the Chinese empire. However, as this declined in importance and power Korea became an area of rivalry between two rising Asiatic powers, the Russian empire and Japan. Japan's victory in the 1904–05 Russo-Japanese War ensured that it would be the dominant foreign power in Korea, and in 1910 Korea formally became part of the Japanese empire. It remained under Japanese control until the end of the Second World War.

In August 1945, Soviet armed forces attacked and defeated Japanese military forces in the northern Chinese province of Manchuria. By the end of August Soviet forces had occupied Manchuria and northern Korea as far south as the 38th parallel. In the same month the USA effectively brought the Pacific war to an end when it dropped atomic bombs on Hiroshima and Nagasaki. US military forces under Lt Gen John R. Hodge occupied Korea south of the 38th parallel from September. Such a division was seen by both the USA and USSR as a temporary arrangement until such time as an agreement could be made to reunite Korea as an independent state. The Korean peninsula, mainly mountainous and approximately 600 miles long and 150 miles wide, was perceived by the USA to be of limited economic and military value.

During Japanese rule, the first signs of modern Korean nationalism began to develop. One important nationalist was born Kim Song-ju, in 1912. His parents were Korean nationalists who fled to China to escape Japanese rule. While living in China, Kim joined the Communist Party and changed his name to **Kim Il-sung**. During the 1930s he fought the Japanese in Korea as a guerrilla. In 1940 he fled Korea and enlisted in the Soviet Army, where he rose to the position of battalion commander. In October 1945 Kim returned to Soviet-occupied North Korea along with several thousand other Korean Communists. In February 1946 he set up the Interim People's Committee of Korea, which was the first stage in creating a Communist government for North Korea.

Another fervent Korean nationalist was **Syngman Rhee**. He was a Christian who had been sent to the USA in 1905 to gain support for Korean independence after the Russo-Japanese War. The US president, Theodore Roosevelt, had acted as mediator in the creation of a peace treaty between the Russians and Japanese at Portsmouth, New Hampshire. Syngman Rhee stayed in the USA, learnt English and developed contacts with the US State Department. In 1945 he was seen as an ideal choice to head a US-backed non-Communist government in South Korea.

By the autumn of 1948, two separate governments had been formed. In September 1948 Soviet troops withdrew from the north and the Democratic Republic of Korea was proclaimed. Kim Il-Sung was the head of its government and he began moving North Korea to a Soviet-style economy. All agriculture was taken under state control and collectivised. The government was a dictatorship, and the police ensured strict one-party control of politics and the media. To all intents and purposes North Korea was a puppet state of the USSR, similar to the Communist-controlled states of eastern Europe.

In the south a postwar administration was established by Lt Gen Hodge. To ensure a rapid re-establishment of order after the Japanese surrender he employed many Koreans who had formerly worked for the Japanese. This caused considerable resentment within South Korea. In December 1945 the USA and USSR agreed to set up a Joint Commission, through which they, not the Koreans, would organise the postwar government. Under the US Military Government in Korea (USAMGIK) opposition turned to strikes, demonstrations and violence. The Daegu Uprising of 1 October 1946 led to the deaths of several student demonstrators opposed to USAMGIK. Even using martial law the US administration found it difficult to control the south. Eventually, by 1948, an anti-Communist strongman appeared who would lead a Korean government in the south: Syngman Rhee.

From 1948 to 1950 the Korean peninsula was home to two governments, each aiming to unite the Korean people under its own rule. In the north Kim Il-sung pressured Soviet leader Josef Stalin to support his desire to unite the peninsula by force. Although initially opposed to the idea, Stalin changed his mind in January 1950. On 30 January 1950 Stalin replied to Kim's demands through the Soviet ambassador to North Korea, Shtykov, stating:

> I understand the unhappiness of comrade Kim Il-sung, but he must understand that such a large matter regarding South Korea...requires thorough preparation. It has to be organised in such a way that there will not be a large risk. If he wants to talk to me on this issue, then I'll always be ready to receive him and talk to him...I am prepared to help him in this matter.

In April 1950 Kim Il-sung visited Moscow and final preparations were made for a Communist invasion of the south.

At 4 a.m. on 25 June 1950, North Korean armed forces crossed the 38th parallel and began the invasion of the south. With several hundred tanks and self-propelled guns supplied by the USSR, more than 200 aircraft supplied by the USSR and flown by Soviet pilots, and a well-trained army of 220,000 men, the North Koreans overran the poorly equipped South Korean forces with ease. At 11 a.m. North Korea formally declared war. Sometimes referred to in South Korea as the 6.25 War (as it began on 25 June), and more widely as the Forgotten War (because it is less prominent in the public consciousness than the Second World War or the later Vietnam War), the conflict was to last 3 years and cost the lives of some 40,000 US, 250,000 North Korean, 200,000 Chinese and 50,000 South Korean soldiers and hundreds of thousands of civilians. It proved to be the first major armed conflict in the Cold War.

The course of the Korean War

When the North Korean army attacked the south, US President Truman was at home in Independence, Missouri, far from Washington, DC. As a result, State Department officials took the initiative as the war unfolded. In New York, a resolution was passed at the UN on 25 June calling for an immediate end to hostilities by the North Koreans. On 26 June Truman announced: 'The United States will vigorously support the effort of the UN Security Council to terminate this serious breach of peace.' To back up this statement Truman ordered the US 7th Fleet to protect Taiwan from Communist attack and US ground and air forces in east Asia to come to South Korea's assistance. On

27 June the UN Security Council adopted a resolution whereby the UN offered South Korea military assistance against the invasion. Fortunately for Truman, the USSR had temporarily withdrawn from the Security Council in protest at the failure of the UN to recognise Communist China and so was not in a position to veto the resolution. On 29 June, US General MacArthur was appointed Commander in Chief of UN forces in South Korea.

The USA took the leading role in persuading the UN to take effective military action in response to the North Korean attack. The majority of the UN forces were provided by the USA, with the second largest contribution coming from the UK. Forces from Canada, Australia, New Zealand, France, Belgium, Greece, Turkey, the Philippines, Colombia, Ethiopia, the Netherlands, South Africa and Thailand also took part.

In the initial phase of the war, from June to September 1950, the North Korean army quickly occupied most of the south. The South Korean army was short of tanks and effective training. The first US troops sent to South Korea from Japan lacked military experience and proved no match for the North Koreans. On 28 June 1950 the North Koreans captured the southern capital, Seoul, and by August they had reduced the US and South Korean military presence to a small area of southeastern Korea, around the city of Pusan.

In September 1950 General MacArthur launched a counteroffensive in a brilliant masterstroke at Inchon, on the western coast of Korea, near Seoul. Operation Chromite was a landing by US amphibious forces behind North Korean lines aimed at cutting off the North Korean forces by advancing across the Korean peninsula. This was a highly risky operation. Amphibious operations were difficult to coordinate, and Inchon's very high tidal range meant that the landings had to be executed with great precision. After a surprise landing on 15 September, US forces quickly established a bridgehead. By 22 September US marines had entered Seoul and the North Korean army was in full retreat, attempting to escape complete encirclement.

The second phase of the war lasted from September to October 1950. MacArthur, with President Truman's backing, made the controversial decision to invade North Korea. This went beyond the initial UN resolution, which concentrated on defending South Korea against aggression. The US-led UN forces quickly overran the North Korean capital of Pyongyang, the first Communist capital to fall to US troops after 1945. By October, the UN forces were approaching the North Korean border with Communist China, at the Yalu River, and US warplanes engaged in combat with North Korean planes in this area.

On 19 October 1950 the war entered a third phase, when approximately 250,000 Chinese troops of the Chinese People's Volunteer Army poured across the Yalu River and attacked UN forces. Surprised and overwhelmed, the latter began a headlong retreat south in the early stages of a bitterly cold Korean winter. It proved to be the longest retreat in US military history. By January 1951 the North Koreans and Communist Chinese had recaptured Pyongyang and Seoul. The UN forces under

MacArthur made a stand against the Communist advance in February 1951, and in the following month recaptured Seoul for a second time. The intervention of Communist China had transformed the war. The Korean War now had the potential to become a Third World War in Asia. Faced with Chinese intervention, and with the Chinese Civil War technically unfinished, MacArthur wanted to broaden the scope of the conflict into a general war.

MacArthur had always found it difficult to submit to the authority of US politicians, regarding himself as more knowledgeable and professional. He abhorred political interference in his military decision making, and has been described as an 'American Caesar'. In particular, he despised President Truman, who had been a haberdasher and had only risen to the rank of captain during the First World War. On 15 October 1950 the two men met for the first time on the US-controlled Pacific island of Guam. When MacArthur greeted Truman he refused to salute his commander-in-chief. Truman in turn detested MacArthur for his arrogance and his thinly disguised support for the opposition Republican Party.

In October 1950 MacArthur was at the height of his popularity. He had overseen the successful postwar reconstruction of Japan and had defeated the North Korean army. However, by March 1951 the Korean War had changed dramatically. With Chinese intervention the war had entered a new, more deadly phase, in which the US-led UN forces faced a long war of attrition in central Korea. MacArthur's suggestion to expand the scope of the war by including Nationalist Chinese troops and attacking Communist China raised the spectre of a nuclear confrontation with the USSR and a global war. In contrast, Truman wanted to end the conflict. On 20 March he informed MacArthur that he was going to propose a cease-fire to the Communists. MacArthur was enraged. On 5 April, he sent a letter to the Republican leader in the US House of Representatives, Joseph Martin, stating that 'there is no substitute for victory' and that the USA should invade North Korea and use Nationalist Chinese troops. This proved to be the last straw for Truman. MacArthur was flagrantly trying to usurp the civilian control of the military. On 11 April 1951 Truman took the difficult and fateful decision to sack MacArthur as UN Supreme Commander. He replaced him with US General Matthew Ridgeway.

MacArthur's sacking was a sensation. Across the USA Republicans were outraged, some even demanding that Truman be impeached and removed from office. When MacArthur returned to the USA he received a hero's welcome in New York City and was invited to address both houses of Congress. His dismissal also fuelled the anti-Communist hysteria instigated by Republican Senator Joseph McCarthy. In retrospect it can be argued that Truman made the right decision, because it led to a limitation of US military activity in the far east. If MacArthur's views on the war had been supported by the US government, the Korean conflict could have escalated into a major Asian, and possibly global, war. However, the dismissal of MacArthur undermined Truman's administration and led directly to the Republican victory in the 1952 presidential election.

The final phase of the Korean War lasted from March 1951 to 27 July 1953. It was a war of attrition running across the peninsula, roughly along the boundary of the 38th parallel. Cease-fire negotiations between North and South Korea began at Kaesong in July 1951 and then transferred to Panmunjom.

The fighting came to an end on 27 July 1953 with an exchange of prisoners of war. However, the Korean War has yet to end officially. Meetings still take place at Panmunjom between North and South Korea, and the border between the two states is regarded as one of the most heavily defended in the world.

The consequences of the Korean War

The impact of the Korean War on the USA

The Korean War was the USA's first major armed conflict after the Second World War. Technically, it was not a war but a UN 'police action'. President Truman had not gone to the US Congress for a declaration of war, which he was required to do under the US Constitution. Instead, military action was sanctioned by the UN Security Council.

The reaction of the UN to North Korean aggression showed clearly that unlike its predecessor, the League of Nations, it was willing to meet force with force. In the end a wide variety of UN member-nations provided military units. Others, such as Chile, provided support facilities.

The war had a significant cost for the USA: 33,600 servicemen died and more than 100,000 were wounded. US servicemen who were captured by the North Koreans and Chinese complained of maltreatment including torture and brainwashing. The Korean War was second only to the Vietnam War for the scale of US casualties in post-1945 conflicts.

In terms of financial impact, US military expenditure rose from 4% of GDP in 1948 to 14% by 1953. This caused inflationary pressure within the USA. It also brought the military expansion recommendations of NSC68 into the realms of reality.

The war had an adverse effect on the Truman administration. When the war began, there was bipartisan support within Congress. However, this began to evaporate with the failure of UN troops to win the war in late 1950. It disappeared completely with the sacking of General MacArthur in April 1951. Questions were raised across the USA. Why had the world's most powerful military nation, in alliance with other UN countries, failed to win? Why had US forces suffered so badly when fighting the Chinese from October 1950? In the late autumn and early winter of 1950–51 US troops had been forced to retreat 300 miles, and in the stalemate of 1951–53 it had been impossible to deliver a knockout blow to the enemy.

Failure to win a decisive victory fuelled anti-Communist hysteria in the USA. Was this failure due to Communist subversion at home? With the loss of China to communism in 1949, and then the stalemate in Korea, Republican Senator Joseph McCarthy was able to exploit the situation for his own benefit. To McCarthy, the US State Department was riddled with Communist sympathisers. Communist supporters in various parts of society were undermining the USA. Otherwise why had the world's greatest military and economic power not won easily?

Truman was so shaken by the Korean stalemate that he decided not to run for president in 1952. Instead, the Democrats chose Adlai Stevenson, a liberal intellectual and the type of person Joseph McCarthy detested. The Republicans chose General **Dwight Eisenhower**, Second World War commander and victor of D-Day and the European campaign of 1944–45. Eisenhower won the 1952 presidential election with relative ease.

To Truman the Korean War had been the application of the strategy of containment to the far east. Korea was now definitely within the US defence perimeter in Asia. Large numbers of US troops were permanently stationed in South Korea from 1953 and have remained there to the present day to deter a possible North Korean attack. From 1951 Truman and his successor began a process which aimed to contain the spread of communism on the world's largest continent. In 1951 the USA signed military agreements with Japan and the Philippines permitting the creation of major US military installations. Okinawa, the main US base in Japan, was within easy flying distance of both Korea and Communist China, while in the Philippines the USA had Clark Air Force Base and the Subic Bay naval facility. In 1951 the USA signed the ANZUS Pact with Australia and New Zealand, a major turning point in Australian and New Zealand foreign policy. Until 1951 both Commonwealth countries had relied on the UK for military protection but now they looked to the USA. In 1954 the USA engineered the creation of the South East Asian Treaty Organisation (SEATO) along the lines of NATO. Its members were the USA, the UK, France, Australia, New Zealand, Thailand, the Philippines and Pakistan, with South Vietnam as an associate member, and its purpose was to counter the threat of communism. With US military alliance commitments extended across Asia, the Korean War was a major factor in the globalisation of the Cold War.

To meet these new commitments the US military budget increased markedly. What some thought was a temporary rise in expenditure during the Korean War became a permanent feature. The US Navy grew from 600 to more than 1,000 vessels during the 1950s. The USA also greatly increased its nuclear capability, exploding a hydrogen bomb in 1952 and developing a nuclear missile capability on land and sea.

By 1960 the USA's military spending had become such a permanent feature that outgoing US President Dwight Eisenhower warned his successor, John F. Kennedy, that the US economy had become heavily dependent on high military expenditure.

The Korean War also brought a reappraisal of US policy with regard to Chinese affairs. Before the war Dean Acheson had not included the Nationalist Chinese-controlled island of Taiwan in the US defence perimeter in Asia. During the war Truman was reluctant to use Nationalist Chinese troops, against General MacArthur's wishes. However, after the war Nationalist China became an ally of the USA in its campaign to contain Communist expansion in Asia. The US 7th Fleet regularly patrolled the Formosa Strait, which separated Communist China from Taiwan. In 1954 the

Table 3 US defence spending, 1950–59

	Defence spending $ billion
1950	18.1
1951	26.4
1952	48.5
1953	56.1
1954	52.1
1955	47.0
1956	47.2
1957	52.8
1958	54.2
1959	54.2

Source: US Department of Commerce; Bureau of Economic Analysis

Communists began shelling two Nationalist-controlled islands off the coast of China, Matsu and Quemoy. The USA made it clear to Communist China that it would not tolerate an invasion of Nationalist Chinese territory. From 1954 to 1972 the USA steadfastly defended Nationalist China against potential Communist aggression. It also refused to support Communist China's application to join the UN.

The impact of the war on the far east

The war had a devastating effect on Korea. Approximately 10% of the population had been killed. The population of North Korea declined from 9 million to 7 million through death and emigration to the south. More than 600,000 homes had been destroyed and what industrial capacity the Koreans had had before the war had largely been destroyed. After the war North Korea developed into a hardline Communist state under Kim Il-sung ('the Great Leader'). The more populous South Korea benefited from US aid and developed into a modern industrial state.

Japan also benefited economically. US demand for trucks and military equipment stimulated the growth of the Japanese economy. By 1954 Japan was earning $4 billion per year from sales of goods to the USA. This helped launch what became known as the Japanese economic miracle during the 1950s and 1960s.

The People's Republic of China lost approximately 150,000 war dead in the conflict. However, its leader Mao Zedong had shown that he could stand up to the greatest military power in the world. The Chinese had prevented the fall of North Korea. Mao's reputation within his own country and in the wider Communist world rose considerably. Following the death of Stalin in March 1953, Mao saw himself as the potential leader of world communism. As a result, the Korean War laid the foundations for the Sino–Soviet split which occurred at the end of the 1950s.

Key figures

Kim Il-sung (1912–94): founding leader of the Democratic People's Republic of Korea (North Korea). Born Kim Sung-ju, he was brought up as a Christian but became a Communist in the 1920s. In 1935 he joined the Northeast Anti-Japanese Army, a Communist force fighting to expel the Japanese from Manchuria, which they had occupied in 1931–32. In the same year he changed his name to Kim Il-sung (which translates as 'come the sun'). He later joined the Soviet Army. When the USSR occupied the northern part of Korea in 1945 Kim became the leader of North Korea's Communists, taking the post of chairman of the Korean Workers' Party from 1949. He helped to set up the North Korean army. By 1950 he was able to persuade Stalin, the Soviet leader, that a Communist invasion of the south would unite Korea under his rule. After the Korean War, Kim established a personal dictatorship in North Korea. Known as 'the Great Leader', he ruled the country as prime minister and then as president until his death in 1994. He was replaced as leader by his son, Kim Jong-il (known as 'the Dear Leader').

Syngman Rhee (1875–1965): first president of South Korea, a post he held from August 1948 to April 1960. Born into an aristocratic family, he was educated in the USA, where he received a PhD from Princeton University. He led South Korea during the Korean War. Although anti-Communist, his regime was hardly a full reflection of democracy. Syngman Rhee ruled South Korea in an authoritarian way.

Dwight Eisenhower (1890–1969): US president from 1953 to 1961. During the Second World War Eisenhower was appointed Supreme Allied Commander for western Europe in the period 1944–45. He commanded Allied forces at D-Day and in the defeat of German forces until 1945. After the war, Eisenhower was appointed the first NATO commander from 1949. During his presidency Eisenhower claimed he would engage in 'roll back', winning back territory lost to communism. However, for most of his presidency he followed Truman's policy of containment.

The USA in southeast Asia, 1954–64

Southeast Asia is an area which today includes the countries of Vietnam, Laos, Cambodia, Thailand, Myanmar, Brunei, Malaysia, Indonesia and the Philippines. Following the conclusion of the Korean War it was an area of important strategic concern to the USA. By 1950 the Philippines was a close ally of the USA. Thailand, Indonesia and Myanmar (then known as Burma) were independent states. However, Malaysia and the area known as Indo-China (comprising Vietnam, Laos and Cambodia) were parts of European empires. Malaysia (then known as the Federation of Malaya) was under British control, while Indo-China was ruled by the French. The

USA feared the expansion of communism into the region. To counter this it became a supporter of colonial regimes fighting to defeat indigenous nationalist movements which had links to communism. Eventually, by the mid-1960s the USA would be drawn into the region militarily, in the American phase of the Vietnam War.

The causes of the conflict in Vietnam

By the outbreak of the Second World War the French had become the colonial masters of Indo-China. They had set up colonial administrations in Vietnam, Laos and Cambodia. When Nazi Germany occupied France in June 1940, Japan took the opportunity to establish military bases in French Indo-China. From 1940 to 1945 Japan occupied the region. In 1941, in a bid to remove the Japanese, a Vietnamese Nationalist organisation called the Vietminh was created. A leading figure in its creation was a young Communist known as **Ho Chi Minh.** From 1941 to 1945 the Vietminh engaged in guerrilla warfare against the Japanese. During this time the Vietminh received supplies from the USA. When the Japanese surrendered, Ho Chi Minh declared Vietnamese independence, in Hanoi, North Vietnam. He used as his example the American Declaration of Independence.

However, in 1945, instead of accepting an independent Vietnam, the western Allies decided to re-establish French colonial rule. Initially there was an uneasy peace between the Vietminh and the French, but this came to an end in 1946, when open warfare broke out. From 1946 to 1954 the Vietminh fought the French. From the American point of view, 1950 marked a transformation in this colonial war. Mainland China, which shared a border with French Indo-China, had become Communist the previous year, and with the outbreak of the Korean War in 1950 the Vietminh were now seen as Communist guerrillas attempting to expand communism into southeast Asia. At the same time, Communist guerrillas were fighting British troops in Malaya. Although traditionally an anti-colonial power, the USA began supporting the French with huge amounts of military aid, spending over $2 billion on military aid at its peak, which represented approximately 80% of the French cost of the war.

In spite of US efforts, the Vietminh increased their activity. By 1953 the Vietminh had a regular army of 250,000 and a militia of 1.8 million, and they harassed French colonial forces across Vietnam. Much of the countryside of northern Vietnam was under their direct control. They set up an alternative administration, with schools and hospitals.

The climax of the war came in 1954 on the borders of Laos and northern Vietnam at Dien Bien Phu. The French established a major military base in the hope of forcing the Vietminh into a set-piece battle, which the French expected to win because of their superior military equipment and firepower. Under **General Giap** the Vietminh surrounded the base and cut it off from supplies in a prolonged siege through the spring of 1954. It was eventually forced to surrender in May 1954, having suffered 7,200 dead and 11,000 captured. This was a major humiliation for the French armed forces and spelt the death knell for French rule in Indo-China.

The French defeat occurred when negotiations for a settlement were taking place in Geneva, Switzerland. Following Dien Bien Phu the French agreed to leave Indo-China. Laos and Cambodia were created as independent, neutral kingdoms. Vietnam was to be temporarily divided along the 17th parallel. To the north of that line Ho Chi Minh created the Democratic Republic of Vietnam, a Communist state. To the south a non-Communist Vietnamese administration was established. The aim was to hold nationwide elections in Vietnam in 1956 as a prelude to reuniting the country.

The impact of French defeat on US policy

Dwight Eisenhower became president in January 1953. His Republican administration had been critical of Truman's Democratic government and its stance on communism. Eisenhower's Secretary of State, John Foster Dulles, did not just want to contain the expansion of communism: he wanted to roll it back. Given the rapid spread of Asiatic communism since 1945, the USA feared that unless a stand was made other countries would fall. In 1954 Eisenhower stated:

> You have a row of dominoes set up, you knock over the first one, and what will happen to the last one is the certainty that it will go over very quickly...Asia, after all, has already lost some 450 million of its peoples to the Communist dictatorship...But when we come to the possible sequence of events, the loss of Indo-China, of Burma, of Thailand, of Malaya and Indonesia following...now you are talking about millions and millions of people.

This 'domino theory' underpinned US policy towards southeast Asia in the 1950s and 1960s.

Eisenhower not only supplied France with money and war materiel but also with advisors. By 1954, 300 US personnel were serving in the **Military Assistance Advisory Group (MAAG)** with the French in Indo-China. Following the 1954 Geneva Accords which ended the French war, MAAG was limited to 342 personnel in South Vietnam.

The USA was displeased with the Geneva Accords, which established a Communist regime in North Vietnam. Eisenhower feared that the planned 1956 Vietnamese elections might give Ho Chi Minh and the Communists a majority. After all, they had led the nationalist struggle to expel the French.

Eisenhower admitted as much in his private diary. The challenge for the Americans was to find an anti-French and anti-Communist Vietnamese nationalist to lead the administration of South Vietnam. In 1954 the head of state of South Vietnam was the Emperor Bao Dai. He was an indolent playboy and puppet ruler under the French. The USA began putting its faith in **Ngo Dinh Diem.** He was a Catholic from a middle-class background who had opposed the French. His religious views made him a fervent anti-Communist.

In 1954 he became prime minister of South Vietnam, and in the following year he ousted Bao Dai and declared himself president of the Republic of South Vietnam. South Vietnam joined SEATO as an associate member.

Although not popular in a country which was predominantly Buddhist, Diem was the best the USA could find to lead South Vietnam. In 1956 he repaid US support by cancelling the planned nationwide elections agreed in the Geneva Accords.

To help Diem build a viable South Vietnamese state, the USA gave him substantial aid of approximately $500 million a year. MAAG also began the task of training a separate South Vietnamese Army known as ARVN (Army of the Republic of Viet Nam). Diem knew that the USA needed him as much as he needed them. Unfortunately for the Americans Diem's government was riddled with corruption and favouritism. As a Catholic in a predominantly Buddhist country, Diem surrounded himself with Catholic advisors and family members.

The USA urged Diem to introduce land reform and end corruption, but to no avail. To anti-Communists in the USA Diem was the frontline defender of freedom. Fellow Catholics such as senators **John F. Kennedy** (known as 'JFK') and Mike Mansfield hailed Diem as an enlightened ruler. Reality was another matter. Diem's brother Ngo Dinh Nhu was made head of state security. He arrested thousands of political opponents, torturing and killing many. With the failure to call elections and a crackdown on political freedom, many saw South Vietnam as no different from the Communist-controlled north.

In 1958 the Communists in the north began equipping Communist guerrillas in South Vietnam. Clashes occurred with the ARVN. Then, in 1960, North Vietnam officially founded the **National Liberation Front (NLF)**, a coalition of nationalist groups under Communist leadership that aimed to overthrow the Diem regime and bring unification with the north. By the time John F. Kennedy won the 1960 presidential election MAAG had 1,600 personnel advising the ARVN.

In addition, Communist guerrillas were attempting to overthrow the neutral government of Laos. When Kennedy met Eisenhower in early 1961 as part of the presidential handover he was warned about the developing crisis in Indo-China and its potential impact on the domino theory.

John F. Kennedy and Indo-China

John F. Kennedy became president at the height of the Cold War. It was widely believed in Washington, DC that the USA faced an international Communist conspiracy. In the first 2 years of his presidency Kennedy faced major crises over Berlin and Cuba, where he was forced to stand up to what he saw as Communist aggression. In his inaugural address in January 1961 he made it clear where he stood, stating:

> *Let every nation know, whether it wishes us well or ill, that we shall pay any price, bear any burden, meet any hardship, support any friend, oppose any foe, in order to assure the survival and the success of liberty.*

In these circumstances, and with this commitment, Kennedy confronted the issue of Indo-China. By 1961 Communist forces, called the Pathet Lao, were attempting to undermine the neutral government of the Kingdom of Laos. In South Vietnam, NLF guerrilla forces were engaged in destabilising the government. Much controversy has surrounded Kennedy's policy in southeast Asia since his assassination in November 1963. On one hand, there are those who believe he did not want the USA to become embroiled in a major war in southeast Asia. Others believe Kennedy's actions made US military involvement under President Lyndon Johnson inevitable.

By the time Kennedy became president the number of US military advisors in South Vietnam had risen to 1,600 from the 342 permitted by the Geneva Accords of 1954. By December 1961 they were up to 3,000, then 10,000 in 1962 and 16,000 in 1963. This was a considerable escalation in US involvement. These advisors provided training for the ARVN. US advisors also acted as helicopter pilots transporting ARVN troops to engage NLF guerrillas. An important part of this force was a new elite contingent called the Green Berets. Kennedy believed that the US armed forces had to develop a specialist guerrilla warfare corps to fight Communist guerrillas on their own terms. South Vietnam was to be the proving ground for these special forces. If successful they would be used across the world wherever the USA faced Communist subversion.

The main area of activity for the Kennedy administration in 1961–62, however, was Laos. The Central Intelligence Agency (CIA) operated a clandestine air supply service to non-Communist forces fighting the Pathet Lao. The CIA also trained and equipped non-Communist Lao troops. The US air force launched secret bombing raids on Pathet Lao positions in the Plain of Jars, in central Laos. In 1962 US negotiators were able to get a cease-fire in Laos with the creation of an all-party neutral administration. Kennedy saw this as a possible solution to his problems in South Vietnam.

To the outside world the Kennedy administration portrayed Diem, the president of South Vietnam, as southeast Asia's strongman and the first line in the defence of freedom against Communist subversion. Privately, however, many of JFK's advisors had deep reservations about Diem. He was seen as corrupt and authoritarian. Attempts were made to assist Diem to defeat the Communist fighters deployed in South Vietnam (known as the Vietcong or VC). Using a policy successfully employed by the British in Malaya against Communist guerrillas, the USA pressured Diem into creating strategic hamlets. These were fortified villages defended by armed guards. However, the strategic hamlets programme proved to be a failure. Diem put his brother Nhu in charge of the programme. Villagers were uprooted from their traditional homes, which caused resentment. Moreover, Nhu established strategic hamlets in areas where Diem could gain more political support rather than areas threatened by the Vietcong.

By early 1963 opposition to Diem was growing across South Vietnam. Communists were joined by Buddhists who despised Diem's Catholic ruling clique. Catholic flags were flown from government buildings and Buddhist religious flags and emblems were banned. The first serious resistance by Buddhists began in the city of Hue in

May 1963. In the ensuing demonstration nine civilians were shot dead by South Vietnamese police. By June 1963 curfews were imposed across the country to stem Buddhist demonstrations. However, in the same month a Buddhist monk, Thich Quang Duc, set himself on fire in front of the presidential palace in Saigon, the capital of South Vietnam. Photographs and television footage of this gruesome event were shown throughout the world. His suicide was followed by similar self-immolation by monks in the following weeks. Demonstrations erupted across South Vietnam. More than 30 people were killed and nearly 1,500 arrested.

By the autumn of 1963 the Kennedy administration had come to the conclusion that Diem was not the solution to South Vietnam's problems, but in fact was himself the problem. Diem's government was alienating large parts of the South Vietnamese population. Also, in spite of US military aid, the ARVN was failing to make an impact on the growth of Communist guerrilla activity. In January 1963, at the Battle of Ap Bac, 2,000 ARVN troops supported by US helicopters failed to defeat a Vietcong force of only 350. The time was fast approaching for a decision to be made about support for Diem. In August 1963 Kennedy appointed Henry Cabot Lodge as US ambassador to South Vietnam. He rapidly came to the conclusion that Diem had to be removed if the USA was to stand any chance of defeating the Vietcong. The CIA began plotting with senior elements of the ARVN to depose Diem, and on 1 November military units staged a coup d'état. Kennedy hoped that Diem would flee the country, but in fact Diem and his close associates were murdered by the army. These events took place only 3 weeks before JFK's own assassination.

By the time of his death, Kennedy's southeast Asian policy was in a mess. Diem was replaced by General Duong Van Minh, who in turn was replaced by General Nguyen Khanh in February 1964. Instead of making the South Vietnamese government stronger, the removal of Diem led to a period of chronic political instability.

Kennedy's unexpected death has left a number of unanswered questions. Was he already planning to withdraw US military support from South Vietnam? According to British historian Lawrence Freedman, in *Kennedy's Wars*, published in 2000, JFK was waiting until he had won the 1964 presidential election before pulling out US troops. Others believe he tried to steer a middle course between the 'hawks' who wanted a big increase in US involvement and the 'doves' who supported withdrawal. It is very difficult to take a precise position on JFK's intentions as so little evidence on his views has been published. To Kennedy, even as late as November 1963, South Vietnam was a sideshow in the Cold War. Far more important was the Soviet threat in Europe and the Castro regime in Cuba. If he had lived to see the disintegration of government in South Vietnam, he might have been forced into greater commitment. As it turned out, however, the problems of a deteriorating political and military position in South Vietnam were left to his successor, Lyndon Johnson.

Glossary

Military Assistance Advisory Group (MAAG): played a major part in training the South Vietnamese Army from 1955 to 1964. It was under a US general and until 1960 had a nominal maximum of 342 members, in line with the Geneva Accords.

National Liberation Front (NLF): the National Front for the Liberation of Vietnam, set up in 1960 with the aim of overthrowing the government of South Vietnam. Its chairman was a non-Communist Saigon lawyer opposed to Diem, but overall the NLF was Communist-dominated. The NLF rebels were also known as the Vietcong.

Key figures

Ho Chi Minh (1890–1969): Vietnamese nationalist leader who helped found the Vietminh and led Vietminh forces against the French from 1946 to 1954. He then became the first leader of North Vietnam. Throughout his life Ho Chi Minh hoped to unify the Vietnamese people under his Communist regime. He supported the creation of the National Liberation Front and the use of North Vietnamese Army troops in South Vietnam. He regarded the Tet Offensive as a failure. He died in 1969. His body now occupies a mausoleum, modelled on Lenin's Moscow mausoleum, in central Hanoi.

Vo Nguyen Giap (1911–): North Vietnamese general, leader of Vietminh forces against the French in the 1946–54 war. Although defeated by the French in the Red River Campaign of 1951–52, he organised the 1954 siege of Dien Bien Phu, which helped to destroy French rule in Indo-China. He then became commander of the North Vietnamese Army. He masterminded Communist strategy in South Vietnam throughout the American War (1965–73). He organised the siege of Khe Sanh in early 1968 and the Tet Offensive. In 1972 he organised the Spring Offensive and in 1975 the Ho Chi Minh Offensive, which conquered South Vietnam. He also became a member of the Politburo, the leading party policy committee in North Vietnam.

Ngo Dinh Diem (1901–63): leader of South Vietnam from 1955 until his assassination in November 1963. A devout Roman Catholic ruling a country with a Buddhist majority, he led an authoritarian, corrupt government dominated by family members. His eldest brother, Ngo Dinh Thuc, was Catholic Archbishop of Hue. Another brother, Nhu, was in charge of state security and ran areas of central South Vietnam like a warlord. Kennedy hoped that his removal would lead to more stable, popular government in South Vietnam. The opposite happened.

John F. Kennedy (1917–63): US president from 1961 to 1963. Kennedy, known as JFK, was a noted anti-Communist, and during his presidency he confronted communism in Berlin and Cuba. In the Cuban Missile Crisis of October 1962 he threatened the USSR with nuclear war if it did not remove its nuclear weapons from Cuba, which it did. In southeast Asia he spent much of his presidency supporting anti-Communist forces in Laos. He maintained US financial and military assistance to the South Vietnamese government, but became disillusioned with Diem's corrupt rule and sanctioned his removal in an ARVN/CIA plot in early November 1963. Kennedy was shaken by the news that Diem had been assassinated. Much controversy surrounded Kennedy's Vietnam policy. Did he intend to commit ground troops or was his military commitment limited to military advisors and financial aid?

The American war, 1964–73

'Johnson's war'?

Following JFK's assassination the USA became increasingly involved in South Vietnam. In March 1965, US marines were sent to defend the Da Nang airbase. This was the beginning of US commitment to all-out war. To most contemporary Americans the Vietnam War became Lyndon Johnson's war. By 1967, anti-war demonstrators were gathering across the USA, chanting 'LBJ, LBJ, how many kids did you kill today?' However, was Lyndon Johnson really committed to extending US military involvement in Vietnam?

On 26 November 1963, just 3 days after Kennedy's assassination, a National Security Action Memorandum stated: 'It remains the central object of the United States in South Vietnam to assist the people and government of that country to win their contest against the externally directed and supported Communist conspiracy.'

From November 1963, when Johnson was sworn in as president, to August 1964 this was the official policy of the USA. The new leader followed Kennedy's policy of supplying financial and military aid to South Vietnam. However, Johnson and his advisors faced increasing problems.

Against a background of unstable government in South Vietnam following Diem's assassination, Vietcong military activity in the south increased. Vietcong forces, supplied with military equipment through the 'Ho Chi Minh trail' guerrilla supply network that linked North and South Vietnam via Laos, increased their attacks on ARVN installations, towns and cities. LBJ received reports that the political and military situation in South Vietnam was deteriorating during the course of 1964. He had set up a Presidential Working Group to study possible options for future US policy in Vietnam. It was chaired by McGeorge Bundy and included representatives of the CIA, the State Department, the Defence Department and the Joint Chiefs of Staff. The Working Group substantiated the view that South Vietnam was politically weak and getting weaker. It suggested that a US aerial bombing campaign against North Vietnam might be the way forward. This would disrupt North Vietnamese supplies to the south and might force the North Vietnamese to the conference table. This act would be supported by the commitment of US ground troops to support the ARVN. The use of vastly superior US military technology would bring the war to an end. The only dissenting voice on the Working Group was George Ball. He thought committing US ground troops would be disastrous, estimating that it would increase troop numbers to 500,000. At the time his predictions were regarded as wildly exaggerated, but in reality George Ball was remarkably accurate in his assessment.

Johnson was aware that he faced a very difficult, deteriorating situation. He had entered national politics just before the Second World War and always believed that the best way to stand up to aggression was with resolute action. He stated on a number of occasions that he opposed appeasing the Communists. Like Eisenhower, LBJ believed in the domino theory. He also did not want to go down in history as the only American president to lose a war. As a result, the USA began to move towards committing itself fully to the Vietnam conflict. Some historians have called this gradual process the Quagmire Theory, in the sense that the USA was drawn into the war gradually, without taking a specific decision to intervene. However, an incident did take place which can be regarded as the moment the US Congress gave LBJ the authority to commit the USA to the conflict.

The Gulf of Tonkin incident, 1964

Between 2 and 4 August 1964, ships of the US Pacific Fleet were patrolling off North Vietnam in the Gulf of Tonkin. Shortly after 1500 hours on 2 August the destroyer USS *Maddox* was attacked 10 miles off the North Vietnamese coast by three North Vietnamese patrol boats which allegedly fired three torpedoes at it, all of which missed. LBJ then agreed that the USS *Maddox* be supported by another destroyer, the USS *C. Turner Joy*. On 4 August the two destroyers approached the North Vietnamese coast, when violent thunderstorms caused their radar to behave erratically. Captain Herrick of the *Maddox* became convinced that he was again under attack and requested air cover from two aircraft carriers operating in the South China Sea, the USS *Constellation* and USS *Ticonderoga*. As soon as LBJ was informed of the second incident he decided to act. Johnson used the 'Gulf of Tonkin incident' to get Congress to pass the Southeast Asia (or Gulf of Tonkin) Resolution. This resolution was rushed through Congress on 6 August 1964 and gave LBJ the authority to take 'all necessary measures' to repel attacks on US forces. Johnson himself later said the resolution was 'like grandma's nightshirt – it covered everything'.

Under the US Constitution only Congress can declare war. However, the president has the authority to protect US citizens abroad. The Gulf of Tonkin Resolution handed Johnson the authority to engage in limited war in southeast Asia. All subsequent US military involvement was substantiated through reference to the Gulf of Tonkin Resolution. Since 1964 much controversy has surrounded the Gulf of Tonkin incident. There is doubt about whether a second North Vietnamese attack actually took place. In 1971, Daniel Ellsberg, a Department of Defense employee, released confidential papers to the *New York Times*. These included Defense Department, CIA and Joint Chiefs of Staff papers. Ellsberg suggested that Congress had been deceived by Johnson and his advisors over the incident. This view was supported in a book by journalist Neil Sheehan, *Bright Shining Lie*, published in 1989.

The timing of the Gulf of Tonkin incident tends to support this view. In August 1964 Johnson was in the middle of a presidential election. He faced an ardent anti-Communist in his Republican opponent, Senator Barry Goldwater of Arizona. The Gulf of Tonkin Resolution allowed LBJ to seem strong and resolute in the face of

Communist aggression. In November 1964 he heavily defeated Goldwater to retain the presidency.

However, there is evidence that the North Vietnamese did attack the USS *Maddox*. At the same time as *Maddox* was patrolling in the Gulf of Tonkin, South Vietnamese special forces were engaged in what were known as De Soto raids along the North Vietnamese coasts, attacking radar and radio installations. Captain Herrick of the USS *Maddox* was unaware of these raids. To the North Vietnamese, *Maddox* and the De Soto raids were part of the same operation, hence the North Vietnamese decision to attack the warship on 2 August.

In the immediate wake of the Gulf of Tonkin Resolution LBJ did not commit US ground troops to South Vietnam, but instead, following the advice of the Working Group, he ordered aerial bombing of selected targets within North Vietnam. In February 1965 these attacks became part of a wider bombing campaign against North Vietnam known as **Operation Rolling Thunder**. This was a systematic attempt to destroy the transport infrastructure of North Vietnam, in particular the supply routes to the Vietcong in the south.

The commitment of US ground troops, 1965

On the morning of 8 March 1965, 3,500 US marines of Amphibious Task Group 76, in landing craft, came ashore on beaches near the city of Da Nang in northern South Vietnam. The marines could have arrived by air at Da Nang airbase or in the deepwater harbour of the city. Instead they landed in a way reminiscent of US marines attacking Japanese-held Pacific islands during the Second World War. They were greeted by the mayor of Da Nang, the media, and Vietnamese girls carrying garlands of flowers. By the end of 1965 Johnson had committed 184,300 US combat troops to South Vietnam.

Johnson decided to commit US ground troops in response to the Vietcong attacks on US military personnel. On 31 October 1964 the Vietcong had attacked US troops at Bien Hoa airbase near Saigon, killing four US personnel and destroying five US bombers. On Christmas Eve 1964 a truck packed with explosives was detonated near the Brink Hotel, Saigon, killing two US military personnel and wounding a further 70. On 7 February 1965 at Camp Holloway, near the Central Highlands city of Pleiku, 300 Vietcong guerrillas attacked the US base with mortars at 2 a.m. Seven Americans were killed and 100 wounded. Johnson raged: 'They are killing our men while they sleep in the night. I can't ask our American soldiers out there to continue to fight with one hand tied behind their backs.' Initially, the marines who landed at Da Nang were expected to defend the airbase and other US military installations in the area. However, within a short time they were patrolling the area with the aim of searching out and destroying the Vietcong. This became the basis of US tactics for much of the Vietnam War.

US military tactics in Vietnam, 1965–68

In June 1964 General **William Westmoreland** became head of the US Military Assistance Command in Vietnam (MACV), replacing General Harkins. Westmoreland was the senior US commander in Vietnam until 1968 and was primarily responsible for US military tactics over that period. Under his leadership US troops adopted search and destroy tactics. According to Westmoreland, US troops would be used most effectively searching out large military concentrations of the enemy and destroying them with their superior firepower. The ARVN would be used to contain Communist guerrilla attacks.

In August 1965, US forces launched Operation Starlite, their first major offensive of the war against Vietcong concentrations near Van Tuong, south of Da Nang. The operation was a complete success and the 1st Vietcong regiment was almost totally destroyed. On 19 October 1965 the first conflict between US forces and the North Vietnamese regular army occurred at the Battle of Ia Drang in the Central Highlands. The US forces, including troops of the 1st Cavalry Division (air mobile) defeated the North Vietnamese. Both these events convinced Westmoreland that the USA could take on and defeat the best Communist troops and also succeed in search and destroy operations. As a result, from 1965 to 1968 the Vietnam War was a series of encounters between highly mobile US forces and Communist forces of the Vietcong and NVA.

The Vietnam War was a helicopter war, with some 5,000 helicopters used by the USA. Thousands of Bell Iroquois helicopters, known as Hueys, were used to transport US troops quickly to areas known for Communist activity. Once Communist forces were located, ground troops were supported by air power. This took many forms. Helicopter gunships fired rockets and aircraft such as A-1 Skyraiders, F-4s and F-5s dropped napalm and bombs on enemy positions.

Unfortunately for the US forces, the Communists adapted quickly to these tactics. When faced with superior US firepower they merely disengaged and melted into the forest which covered much of South Vietnam.

To deter incursions from the north, the USA created a system of unmanned detection and obstacle devices, known as the McNamara Line (after **Robert McNamara**), just south of the Demilitarised Zone (DMZ) which divided North from South Vietnam along the 17th parallel. It also set up military bases in strategic areas across Vietnam. The aim of these bases was to provide helicopter and artillery support to US ground troops. US bases became targets for night attacks by Communist forces, usually using mortars and rockets.

A major campaign was launched against the Ho Chi Minh trail. US special forces planted electronic devices along parts of the trail to monitor Communist transport activity. Then B-52 bombers launched 'Operation Arc Light' attacks. A B-52 was capable of dropping bombs that would obliterate an area 1 km long and half a kilometre wide. After the war the North Vietnamese admitted that Arc Light attacks had had a devastating effect.

As the Communists used the forest cover of Indo-China to hide their transport trails and military movements, the USA responded with Operation Ranch Hand. This was a concerted campaign to defoliate large areas of forest using a chemical called Agent Orange, which contained high levels of dioxin. Operation Ranch Hand was highly controversial. It did succeed in destroying the foliage of tall trees, but once sunlight reached the remaining shrubs these grew in profusion. Agent Orange also poisoned the soil and resulted in the deaths of livestock and birth deformities among Vietnamese peasants. Exposure to Agent Orange enhanced the growth of cancers, and many US personnel exposed to it died subsequently from leukaemia and other cancers, including the son of Elmo Zumwalt, the senior US naval commander in southeast Asia.

To most American servicemen in Vietnam, search and destroy missions were essentially 'chasing Charlie' (Charlie being a slang term for the Vietcong) across the countryside, with little evidence that the US and South Vietnamese forces were actually winning over extra territory.

In 1967 the CIA began the Phoenix Programme, which lasted until 1972. The aim was to take on the Vietcong at their own game. This was a programme for the pacification of South Vietnam through the removal and elimination of Communists and their supporters. Large militias of **Montagnard** troops were created to hunt down Communists in the Central Highlands. Campaigns of abduction, assassination and torture of Communists took place. Tens of thousands of suspected Communists were killed. After the war the USA was accused of human rights violations because of the methods it used during the Phoenix Programme. However, North Vietnamese sources claimed after the war that the programme had been highly effective in limiting Communist influence within South Vietnam.

Some of the USA's allies supported its attempts to bolster the South Vietnamese government: Australia, for example, sent combat troops. In January 1966, in Operation Crimp, US and Australian forces launched an offensive against Vietcong positions in the 'Iron Triangle', an area northeast of Saigon where Communist forces were known to be active. It was also known for a vast network of tunnels which housed Vietcong hospitals, supply dumps, dormitories and food supplies. Throughout the war the USA and its allies attempted to close down this Vietcong operation. In 1967 Operation Cedar Falls destroyed more than 11,000 bunkers and 525 tunnels and captured large quantities of rice, uniforms and medical supplies. However, the Vietcong continued to operate from underground complexes throughout the war. Today some of these tunnel complexes can be visited at Cu Chi.

The USA was also supported by South Korean troops and support forces from New Zealand and the Philippines. The UK was asked to send troops but refused. Along with the USSR, the UK was one of the guarantors of the Geneva Accords of 1954 and felt its role ought to be one of mediation.

Although its individual engagements with the enemy usually ended in military success, the USA did not seem to be making much overall headway. There were successes in the Mekong Delta and around Saigon, but by the end of 1967 there was little sign of impending Communist defeat. However, General Westmoreland continued to give US government officials optimistic reports on progress, and in December 1967 he even predicted a US victory in 1968. This did not, however, stop him requesting more troops for South Vietnam.

Vietcong and North Vietnamese tactics, 1965–68

Westmoreland's optimism did not seem to match the reality on the ground in South Vietnam. The Vietcong and the NVA were elusive enemies. The Vietcong followed military tactics similar to those employed by the Vietminh against the French in 1946–54 and reflecting the weaponry, military training and logistical support available. Vietcong soldiers were usually peasant farmers who had either volunteered or were forced to join. It is difficult to arrive at an accurate figure of Vietcong numbers in the war, but in 1965 there were between 50,000 and 80,000.

Training was extremely limited. Recruits were taught to fire the standard Vietcong infantry weapon, the Soviet-made AK-47 assault rifle, as well as mortars and rockets. The weaponry supplied to the Vietcong either came from North Vietnam through the Ho Chi Minh trail or was captured from ARVN and US forces. Vietcong sympathisers in areas such as Saigon docks simply stole incoming US equipment. Much of the North Vietnamese equipment had originally come from the USSR or Communist China.

In addition to military weapons training, Vietcong recruits were taught how to construct booby traps. These varied widely, from tripwires across forest trails linked to hand grenades or mines, to intricate covered holes filled with sharpened and poisoned bamboo shoots known as punji sticks. During the war the most common cause of battlefield injuries sustained by US troops was mines and booby traps.

Faced with the huge superiority of American firepower, the Vietcong employed guerrilla warfare tactics. The ultimate aim of such tactics was to wear down US morale and force a withdrawal from Vietnam. Many Vietcong recruits were peasant farmers during the day and soldiers at night. Most Vietcong attacks on US and ARVN bases took place after dark. A common phrase among US **grunts** during the war was: 'We control the day but Charlie [the Vietcong] controls the night.'

Vietcong tactics also involved attempts to destroy the local administration of the South Vietnamese government, for example by assassinating local officials. To sustain their fight the Vietcong forced villages to hand over food and money under the threat of violence. A more effective tactic was to establish a Communist local government structure in the countryside. In many areas villages experienced South Vietnamese administration during the day, but in the evening these officials went back to towns and cities to be replaced by Vietcong administrators. The map of Communist control in South Vietnam therefore varied widely between the hours of daylight and night-time.

Although the Vietcong's main areas of strength were in the countryside, there were also supporters in the towns and cities. Throughout the war the capital, Saigon, was subjected to constant terrorist attacks. These involved car bombs, drive-by shootings and the occasional rocket and mortar attack. One of the Vietcong aims was to ensure that nowhere in South Vietnam was free from Communist attack.

When faced with a direct US or ARVN assault, many Vietcong units simply disengaged and fled the area, awaiting a more propitious moment to attack. As a result, many Vietcong attacks were ambushes or hit-and-run raids. The impact of Vietcong tactics was to ensure that the war did not have a clear front line, apart from the DMZ between North and South Vietnam.

An increasingly important element in the Communist forces in South Vietnam was formed by members of the regular North Vietnamese Army (NVA). By the time the USA committed ground troops in March 1965 there were three NVA regiments, numbering 6,000 troops, operating within South Vietnam. They had arrived via the Ho Chi Minh trail. By 1967, NVA numbers had risen to 80,000 out of a combined Communist military strength of 300,000. Both NVA and Vietcong forces received orders and direction from North Vietnam, in particular from General Vo Nguyen Giap, the victor of Dien Bien Phu in 1954 against the French. He also masterminded much of the Communist campaign in the 1960s. Giap tended to use Vietcong formations for small-scale guerrilla warfare, while NVA forces were used for large-scale assaults on ARVN and US forces.

The first major confrontation between US and NVA forces came in the Battle of Ia Drang in late October/early November 1965. Although the US forces suffered heavy casualties they defeated the NVA. The battle was the subject of a Hollywood film, *We Were Soldiers*, starring Mel Gibson.

By the end of 1967 the Communists had large numbers of troops in South Vietnam and controlled large areas of the country, mainly along the Cambodian and Laotian borders and in the Mekong Delta. General Giap and the members of the North Vietnamese Politburo believed the time had come for a major offensive against the South Vietnamese government and US forces in early 1968. It was hoped the offensive would precipitate an uprising which would lead to the collapse of South Vietnam and US withdrawal. At the same time General Westmoreland was reporting to his superiors in Washington, DC that the USA and ARVN were on the verge of military success. Large numbers of Vietcong had been killed in 1966 and 1967. US aerial bombing was damaging North Vietnam's transport infrastructure and Vietcong bases within South Vietnam.

Who was right?

Glossary

Operation Rolling Thunder (1965–68): US aerial bombing campaign against North Vietnam, aimed at destroying the North Vietnamese transport infrastructure and supply routes to Communist forces in South Vietnam. US President Lyndon Johnson brought the operation to an end in 1968, in the hope that this would lead to peace talks.

Although Operation Rolling Thunder did cause disruption it did not achieve its main aims. The chief seaport and supply route in North Vietnam, Haiphong, was not attacked.

Montagnard: mountain tribes living in Vietnam's Central Highlands, including the Bahnar, Jarai, Mnong and Rhade. These were not ethically Vietnamese, and many sided with US forces against the Vietcong. The CIA recruited Montagnard tribesmen to form anti-Communist militias.

grunts: slang term used in the Vietnam War to describe front-line US enlisted men.

Key figures

Robert McNamara (1916–): US Defense Secretary under Presidents Kennedy and Johnson. Robert McNamara was a highly successful chief executive of the Ford Motor Company before joining JFK's government. Regarded as one of the 'best and brightest' who formed Kennedy's cabinet, he was a major supporter of US commitment to South Vietnam. He virtually ran US policy on Vietnam until his departure from the Defense Department in August 1968.

William Westmoreland (1914–2005): US military commander in South Vietnam from 1964 to 1968. Westmoreland adopted the search and destroy tactics used by US forces. He was heavily criticised for sending optimistic reports concerning US military progress. The Tet Offensive took him by surprise. He left his post in August 1968 after the US Congress refused to sanction his request for increased troop numbers. For the rest of his life Westmoreland attempted to justify his tactics and command in South Vietnam.

The Tet Offensive: a turning point?

Tet, the Vietnamese New Year, is the major holiday and time for celebration. US servicemen said Tet was like Christmas, New Year's, Thanksgiving and the Fourth of July all in one. Vietnamese return to their ancestral homes and celebrate Tet with their families. In previous years during the Vietnam War a truce had been observed over the Tet holiday, and 1968 was to follow this pattern — with one exception, the US Marine Corps base at Khe Sanh.

The siege of Khe Sanh

Khe Sanh was the US Marine Corps base in the extreme northwest of South Vietnam, between the DMZ and the Laotian border. Much controversy surrounds the North Vietnamese decision to lay siege to Khe Sanh. General Vo Nguyen Giap has stated that he wanted to cause a major military diversion for US forces during the lead-in to the Tet Offensive. Giap hoped that a Communist attack on Khe Sanh would draw

US forces away from the towns and cities which were to be the main targets of the Communist offensive. During the 77-day siege the USA diverted 30,000 men to the Khe Sanh area, so in this sense he succeeded. Giap deployed four NVA divisions supported by two artillery regiments with 130 mm and 152 mm artillery and two armoured units. This amounted to approximately 15,000 to 20,000 men.

The attack on Khe Sanh began on 21 January 1968. The base was finally relieved on 14 April. During that time heavy fighting surrounded the base, with the NVA attempting to gain control of high ground at Hill 881N and Hill 881S. The base was constantly under artillery, rocket and mortar bombardment. Unfortunately for the defenders, the NVA attack on the first day ignited an ammunition dump, sending 1,500 tonnes of ammunition sky high and destroying helicopters, tents and buildings.

The attack and siege sent shock waves through the White House. President Johnson feared the USA was facing a repeat of the siege of Dien Bien Phu, when 11,000 French paratroops were besieged for 56 days and eventually captured. LBJ even had a model of Khe Sanh constructed and placed in the White House basement so he could watch how the siege developed. Khe Sanh became for LBJ and the US media a test of will. If Khe Sanh fell it would be such a blow to US morale that it might undercut the whole US operation in South Vietnam. At the height of the siege it was rumoured that LBJ and the Joint Chiefs of Staff were contemplating using tactical nuclear weapons to break the siege, a claim denied by General Wheeler, head of the armed forces. Instead the USA launched Operation Niagara, a massive conventional bombing campaign around the base. Niagara I was a comprehensive intelligence-gathering exercise to ascertain the positions of NVA forces building up around Khe Sanh. Niagara II began on 21 January with round-the-clock bombing. Within 24 hours of the start of Niagara II more than 600 airstrikes were launched by air force, marine and navy squadrons. B-52 bombers from bases in Thailand and on the Pacific island of Guam were involved in 49 of these airstrikes. At night AC-47 gunships maintained the pressure. By the end of the siege the USA had launched 24,000 air attacks around Khe Sanh.

During the siege the NVA made no attempt to overrun the marine base. The relief of Khe Sanh was regarded in the US media as a vindication of US involvement in South Vietnam. The NVA had failed to create a second Dien Bien Phu. However, much to the astonishment of many Americans, the marines abandoned their Khe Sanh base later in 1968, stating that it was no longer required.

The Tet Offensive in the cities

On 30 January 1968, the first day of the Tet truce and 9 days after the start of the siege of Khe Sanh, Vietcong forces launched a major offensive across the whole of South Vietnam. The aim was to spark off a national uprising which would cause the collapse of the South Vietnamese government. By 1 February Saigon had been attacked along with 36 of the 44 provincial capitals, five of the six cities and 64 of the 242 district capitals. More than 84,000 Vietcong soldiers had appeared, seemingly from nowhere to the shock and horror of the US command in South Vietnam. In Saigon the Vietcong attacked the ARVN headquarters, the Independence Palace, the national broadcasting station, the Vietnamese navy headquarters and the South Korean and Philippine embassies. The highlight of the Saigon offensive was the attack on the US embassy in Thong Nhat Boulevard, regarded as the most heavily defended building in South Vietnam. Nineteen Vietcong attacked the embassy, killing two marine guards. Although all 19 Vietcong were killed, news footage of this attack appalled Americans who watched the Tet Offensive unfold on prime-time television at home.

Outside the capital another major Vietcong attack occupied the citadel in the middle of the ancient Vietnamese capital of Hue in the north of the country.

ARVN and US forces had to engage in house-to-house fighting to dislodge the Vietcong. It was not until 25 February that the citadel was finally recaptured. Large parts of Hue and the historic citadel suffered extensive damage.

By the end of February the Tet Offensive had been contained, although Vietcong attacks continued until September 1968. General Westmoreland claimed that 37,000 Communists had been killed. Subsequent evidence puts the figure closer to 50,000. The USA lost 2,000 dead and the ARVN 11,000. Untold thousands of civilians died, caught up in the fighting and bombing.

It is clear that the Tet Offensive was a major military defeat for the Communists. The hoped-for national uprising failed to materialise. In fact the brutality of the Communists alienated many Vietnamese. After the offensive, mass graves were uncovered in Hue, containing the bodies of thousands killed by the Communists for being sympathisers with the South Vietnamese government. President Thieu of South Vietnam felt confident enough to order a general mobilisation against the Communists in June 1968.

Politically, however, the Tet Offensive was a disaster for the Americans. General Westmoreland and officials at the State Department and Department of Defence had been telling the American people that the US forces were on the verge of victory in January 1968. Then, on their televisions, Americans saw the Vietcong attack virtually every major city in South Vietnam and even the US embassy. Americans were also put off by scenes of civilian death and material destruction shown nightly on the television. Vietnam was the first ever televised war, with all the horror of war brought into American living rooms. Many were appalled by the brutality shown by the South Vietnamese authorities against Communists. A press photograph showed Saigon police chief Nguyen Ngoc Loan shooting a suspected Vietcong soldier through the head with a revolver.

Television reporting took on a disproportionate role in influencing US opinion. The most famous news anchorman in the USA in 1968 was Walter Cronkite of CBS. When news of the attack on the American embassy reached the USA, Cronkite announced: 'What the hell is going on? I thought we were winning this war.' Cronkite flew to Saigon to view the Tet Offensive at first hand. On 27 February, on his return, he announced on CBS television that he was 'more certain than ever that the bloody experience of Vietnam is to end in a stalemate'. Watching the broadcast, President Johnson stated: 'If I've lost Walter, I've lost Mr Average Citizen.'

The impact of the Tet Offensive was felt in other ways in the USA. Presidential elections were to take place in 1968, and on 12 March the first Democratic Party primary election, to decide who was to be the presidential candidate, was held in New Hampshire. Senator Eugene McCarthy, a virtually unknown national figure, came second to President Johnson in the poll. McCarthy was an anti-war candidate and the result caused a sensation. On 21 March the *New York Times* published a report by General Westmoreland to LBJ in January which suggested the USA had been taken completely by surprise in the Tet Offensive. The following day Johnson decided to replace Westmoreland as US commander in June. He was to be replaced by his deputy General **Creighton Abrams**.

The greatest US casualty of the Tet Offensive was President Johnson. Three years after US ground troops had been committed to South Vietnam, the USA seemed to be nowhere nearing winning the war. Anti-war opposition gathered at home. His approval rating as president dropped alarmingly and the anti-war Eugene McCarthy had undermined Johnson's authority in his own Democratic Party. On 31 March Johnson made a live national television broadcast about the war. At the end of the broadcast he announced he would not seek re-election as president. He also announced a limitation in bombing North Vietnam and stated that for the remainder of his presidency he would try to get a negotiated settlement.

After the Tet Offensive virtually all major US politicians aimed to get a US withdrawal by negotiation. The beginning of the end of US involvement in South Vietnam had come.

US opposition to the war

As the Vietnam War progressed and US military involvement grew, opposition to the war within the USA developed. With no end of the fighting in sight and US casualties mounting, Americans began to question their country's involvement.

Between 1965 and 1973 some 2,700,000 Americans served in Vietnam. The vast majority were conscripts who faced compulsory military service under the Selective Service System, known as the Draft. A typical tour of duty in Vietnam was just under 1 year. Many Americans attempted to avoid the Draft. Some fled to Canada and Sweden to escape it completely. Others claimed college deferment, which allowed them to attend college first before being drafted. Others claimed to be conscientious objectors opposed to war. Others simply burnt their draft cards, refused to serve and faced imprisonment.

Perhaps the most famous conscientious objector in the Vietnam War was world heavyweight boxing champion Muhammad Ali. As a Black Muslim he claimed exemption from the war. He also felt that with racial discrimination at home, African Americans should not fight to defend what he saw as racist America, stating: 'No

Vietcong ever called me nigger.' Ali paid dearly for his stance on the war: he was stripped of his world heavyweight title.

A major area of opposition was among university students. The organisation Students for a Democratic Society, formed in 1960, became a major centre of anti-war opposition. University sit-ins against the war began to develop by 1967.

The biggest impact on opposition to the war at home came with the Tet Offensive. Anti-war demonstrators began to support peace candidates such as Eugene McCarthy. Later, in 1968, Senator Robert Kennedy (JFK's younger brother) decided to run for the Democratic Party nomination for the presidency. He won popular support for his opposition to the war and his demand for a peace settlement. His assassination in Los Angeles in June 1968 robbed the anti-war movement of a national leader but didn't stop opposition.

A major anti-war demonstration, which became a riot, occurred at the Democratic Party National Convention in Chicago in August 1968. Running battles took place between the Chicago police and rioters.

The USA was also plagued by racial tensions throughout 1968. Martin Luther King was assassinated by a white man in April 1968. King had become a major opponent of the war by 1967. His assassination led to widespread rioting across the USA. National Guardsmen had to defend government buildings in Washington, DC against attack.

Anti-war opposition at home undermined military morale in Vietnam. Racial tensions affected US forces. Drug-taking, attacks on officers and unwillingness to fight became more common from 1968.

The height of the anti-war demonstration movement occurred at Kent State University, Ohio, in May 1970. Following the announcement of the US and ARVN invasion of Cambodia, students demonstrated on campus and were confronted by members of the Ohio State National Guard. Faced with serious rioting, the National Guard used tear gas. When they ran out of tear gas they used bullets to quell the riot. Four students were shot dead: Allison Krause, Jeffrey Miller, William Schroeder and Sandra Lee Sheuer. Ten students were wounded. The shootings at Kent State were followed by strikes and sit-ins in universities across the USA. The Kent State incident put great pressure on President Nixon to end the war.

Key figures

Creighton Abrams (1914–74): US general, commander in South Vietnam from 1968 to 1972. He began changing the deployment of US troops, dividing their units into smaller groups to defend villages against Communist attack. During his command the policy of Vietnamisation was introduced. He had to contend with the My Lai massacre trial of Lt William Calley, which caused a worldwide sensation. He left his post in 1972 to become Army chief of staff. He was replaced by General Frederick Weyand for the final year of US involvement in South Vietnam.

Nixon and Vietnamisation

In 1968 Republican **Richard Nixon** narrowly defeated Democrat Hubert Humphrey to win the presidential election. During the campaign Nixon stated that he had a plan that would end the war and bring 'peace with honor' for the USA. On taking office in January 1969, Nixon followed a twin-track policy on Vietnam. He would continue negotiations with the North Vietnamese which had begun in Paris during the last days of LBJ's presidency. He would also withdraw US troops and hand over increasing responsibility for fighting the war to the ARVN. The Vietnamisation of the war would maintain a non-Communist government in South Vietnam and would end US opposition by staging US troop withdrawals. This policy was announced by Defense Secretary Melvin Laird on 1 April 1969. By the end of that month US troop levels reached their peak, at 543,400. The first reduction of 20,000 was announced by Nixon on 8 June. Numbers subsequently began to drop, until by 1972 most US service personnel had left.

Invasion of Cambodia, 1970

From 1969 the war saw more joint actions by US and ARVN forces. Following the Tet Offensive, the NVA took over from the Vietcong as the main Communist force. However, the strength of Communist attacks did not decrease. US advisors argued that the most effective action against the Communists would be to take out their headquarters, known as COSVN and believed to be in neutral Cambodia. Nixon was advised that the best way to end the war was to extend it to Cambodia. By early 1970 plans were put in place to invade Cambodia from South Vietnam and to replace the Cambodian leader, Prince Sihanouk, with a pro-western military government.

On 18 March 1970 Sihanouk was overthrown in a military coup led by General Lon Nol while he was on a visit to Communist China. By 27 March, ARVN forces had attacked suspected Communist bases within Cambodia, while B-52 bombers launched major air raids on Cambodian targets. A full-scale invasion of Cambodia began on 27 April.

The US invasion of Cambodia caused uproar at home. Nixon had agreed to the secret bombing of Cambodia and Laos without informing Congress. His invasion seemed to run counter to his public announcements of troop withdrawals and a de-escalation of the war. The Cambodian invasion also sparked off a civil war in Cambodia. Forces opposed to Lon Nol were led by a small Communist group called the Khmer Rouge. By 1975 they had overrun the capital and instituted a Communist regime, which within 4 years took the lives of one-third of the population in the notorious 'killing fields' of Cambodia.

The Spring Offensive, 1972

The biggest test of Nixon's Vietnamisation policy came in March 1972, when the NVA launched a major invasion of the south. Four NVA divisions attacked Quang Tr province in the northern part of South Vietnam. The USA retaliated with intensive bombing attacks on NVA forces and on North Vietnam. This included direct attacks on the capital, Hanoi, and the main seaport, Haiphong, under the code name Operation Linebacker I. By 5 June North Vietnam admitted that Linebacker I was having a severe effect on the economy, and in the same month ARVN forces began to turn the tide in the Spring Offensive. By 23 July the NVA was in control of only two major towns in South Vietnam. Vietnamisation, supported by massive US air attacks, seemed to have been successful.

However, the key aspect of Nixon's policy was a negotiated peace.

The Paris Peace Agreement, 1973

The peace negotiations which brought an official end to the US involvement in Vietnam lasted from 1968 to 1973. Throughout the talks the North Vietnamese, led by their chief negotiator Le Duc Tho, insisted on Communist involvement in any future government of South Vietnam. This would be a prelude to the reunification of Vietnam under a Communist government. The South Vietnamese side, led by President Nguyen Van Thieu, consistently refused this request. From January 1969 the main US negotiator was **Henry Kissinger**, the National Security Advisor, who worked closely with President Nixon.

A key US tactic was to isolate North Vietnam from its major allies, the USSR and Communist China. In 1969 Nixon began to develop a détente policy towards the USSR, then led by **Leonid Brezhnev**. Both sides started talks to limit the growth of nuclear weapons. Exchange visits of politicians, diplomats and cultural groups occurred. The highlight of these negotiations was the signing of the Strategic Arms Limitation Treaty in 1972. In the same year Nixon visited Communist China and met **Chairman Mao**. This brought to an end the animosity which had prevailed between the two states since the Communists' 1949 victory in the Chinese Civil War. The USA supported Communist China's admission to the UN. These developments greatly improved US relations with the world's biggest Communist states and helped pave the way for peace in Vietnam.

The Paris peace talks continued, but the USA broke off negotiations when the north invaded the south in the Spring Offensive of 1972. Later that year the North Vietnamese began to obstruct negotiations, and Nixon launched the Linebacker II raids to put pressure on them to reach agreement. For 12 days from 18 December 1972, except Christmas Day, the USA launched massive air raids on the north, and on Hanoi and Haiphong in particular. During Linebacker II the USA dropped 20,400 tonnes of bombs on the north, causing 1,000 deaths and the disruption of transport and electricity supply. The USA lost 26 B-52 bombers to SAM-7 surface-to-air missiles. On 8 January 1973 the North Vietnamese returned to the Paris negotiating table.

An agreement was reached on 23 January 1973. It was signed by the USA, North Vietnam, South Vietnam and the Provisional Revolutionary Government of South Vietnam, which represented the Vietcong. Under the agreement all prisoners of war would be exchanged, and US and allied military forces withdrew. NVA forces did not withdraw, but a cease-fire was agreed between the government of South Vietnam and the Vietcong. This led to a division of South Vietnam into Communist-controlled and non-Communist-controlled areas. The job of tracking down and repatriating lost prisoners of war was given to the Four Party Joint Military Commission (FPJMC), based in Saigon. The peace agreement was overseen by the International Commission of Control and Supervision, which comprised representatives of Canada, Indonesia, Hungary and Poland (two Communist and two non-Communist states). The USA also promised millions of dollars in aid for reconstruction, but this was never paid.

Nixon claimed he had brought his country 'peace with honor'. Henry Kissinger and Le Duc Tho received the Nobel Peace Prize. In fact the peace deal was very similar to the one offered by the North Vietnamese in the autumn of 1968. Since that time a further 25,000 US troops had died, Cambodia had been invaded and North Vietnam had been devastated by aerial bombing.

Key figures

Richard Nixon (1913–94): US president from 1969 to 1974. A Republican, Nixon won a narrow victory over his Democrat rival Hubert Humphrey in the presidential election of 1968. He began the process of Vietnamisation of the war and the gradual withdrawal of US troops. His most controversial acts involved the neutral states of Laos and Cambodia. In Operation Menu he ordered the secret bombing of these two states in an attempt to destroy Communist bases and supply routes. In 1970 he ordered the invasion of Cambodia. His international diplomacy, aimed at improving US relations with the USSR and Communist China, helped to isolate North Vietnam diplomatically. He claimed he had achieved 'peace with honor' in the peace agreement of January 1973. He was forced to resign from office in August 1974, as media and congressional investigations uncovered illegal activities during his re-election as president in 1972.

Henry Kissinger (1923–): major foreign policy advisor to Presidents Nixon and Ford in the period 1969 to 1977. He was the main US peace negotiator and engaged in secret diplomacy as a prelude to improving US relations with the USSR and Communist China.

Leonid Brezhnev (1906–82): leader of the USSR from 1964 until his death in 1982. With Nixon he was responsible for developing the policy of détente.

Mao Zedong (1893–1976): ruler of Communist China from 1949 to his death in 1976.

The end of the Vietnam War, 1973–75

From 1973 to 1975 an uneasy peace prevailed in South Vietnam between the non-Communist and Communist governments. In the USA, from 1973 to August 1974, the nation was gripped by the Watergate scandal in which Nixon was accused of engaging in illegal acts such as wiretapping against political opponents. In August 1974 he became the only US president to resign from office. During the Watergate scandal the US Congress began to limit any future US military involvement in Vietnam. In November 1973 Congress passed the War Powers Act, which reversed the Gulf of Tonkin Resolution and greatly limited the president's power to commit US troops abroad. Congress also slashed US financial support to the government of South Vietnam.

On 4 March 1975 the NVA began a major offensive in the Central Highlands. By 13 March it had captured Ban Me Thuot, capital of Dac Lac province, and in so doing it threatened to split the ARVN forces defending central South Vietnam. By the end of March, NVA units had overrun Quang Tri, Hue and Da Nang. Without US air support, the ARVN forces began to collapse. President Thieu ordered his forces to abandon most of the northern part of South Vietnam. On 9–10 April the ARVN made a last stand at Xuan Loc, north of Saigon, but to no avail. Meanwhile, in Cambodia on 14 April Khmer Rouge forces captured the capital Phnom Penh.

On 21 April President Thieu resigned, to be replaced by President Huong. By 25 April Thieu had fled the country and on 28 April, with NVA forces closing on Saigon, President Huong resigned. He was replaced as president by General Duong Van Minh, who transferred political power to the Communists on 30 April. At just after midday a T-54 tank of the NVA broke down the gates of the South Vietnamese presidential palace. South Vietnam had ceased to exist as an independent state.

The last American personnel were airlifted out by plane and helicopter in the last days of April to the US fleet in the South China Sea. As US aircraft carriers did not have space to store all the helicopters, Americans watched on their televisions as US helicopters were pushed over the side into the sea. These were the final harrowing images of the USA's involvement in Vietnam.

Why did the USA fail to win in Vietnam?

Some 2,700,000 US troops served in Vietnam. They were the armed forces of the most advanced military power on earth. The war cost the USA over $145 billion at 1974 prices. The USA dropped 10 million tonnes of bombs and shells and killed approximately 900,000 of the enemy. Yet it still lost. Why?

Since 1975 a variety of explanations has been given for the US failure to win in Vietnam. First, it has been argued that US direct military involvement came too late.

The government of South Vietnam was already collapsing by March 1965. All US involvement achieved was to delay the collapse by a decade. The South Vietnamese government failed to win sufficient hearts and minds to survive. It failed to introduce land reform and was thoroughly corrupt. Promotion to high military command in the ARVN was based on political favouritism rather than ability. ARVN officers were generally poor in quality and had little rapport with their men. Officers tended to come from urban backgrounds, while the rest of the army comprised peasant farmers. In 1972 South Vietnam only survived the Communist Spring Offensive through the deployment of massive US aerial bombing.

Another view involves US military tactics. General Westmoreland has been severely criticised for adopting search and destroy tactics. Opponents of these tactics suggest that counter-insurgency operations would have worked much better. Throughout the war the US government claimed an important aspect of its policy was to win the hearts and minds of the Vietnamese people. This it failed to do. In 1969, US policy was gravely undermined by the announcement that US infantry had engaged in a massacre of Vietnamese civilians at My Lai the previous year. The subsequent court martial of Lt William Calley and his conviction for war crimes undermined the US position across the world.

The type of warfare employed during the war did not suit US superiority in military equipment or the type of soldier that characterised the US forces. South Vietnam was a heavily wooded country. It was difficult to locate and attack enemy forces, which used the terrain to their advantage. Most of the US troops who fought in Vietnam were conscripts who had to serve a 350-day tour. The vast majority had no desire to be in the army, and still less to be in Vietnam. They lacked jungle warfare experience and most knew no Vietnamese beyond a few basic words. These troops yearned for the day when they would return to the USA. They had little idea of which Vietnamese were the Communist enemy and which were innocent civilians. As opposition to the war grew at home, military morale suffered in Vietnam. Alcohol and drug abuse became commonplace from 1968. The US forces were also divided by racial tensions between white and African-American troops. When Vietnam veterans returned home, many were shunned or accused of being baby-killers.

By contrast, the Communist forces knew how to live and fight in jungle conditions. They were fighting for their independence from foreign occupation. As a result, although Communist forces suffered heavy casualties they possessed far higher morale than US forces.

US military authorities were so confident of victory in Vietnam that they allowed the media unrivalled access to war zones. As a result, US television audiences saw a daily dose of US troops burning villages, dropping napalm and destroying the countryside. The press and television played a very negative role in the perception of the war within the USA and around the world. These perceptions fuelled anti-war protests and undermined the US government's claim that it was defending freedom against Communist oppression.

The USA's failure to win can also be explained by a lack of political resolve. Johnson tried to fight a limited war in southeast Asia which would not impinge too greatly on government expenditure and military resources. However, by 1967 the Vietnam War was becoming so expensive that Johnson was forced to divert money away from his Great Society social programmes. By 1968 he faced the prospect of calling up the military reserve forces, which would have been politically unpopular.

US forces that served in Vietnam complained that they were forced to fight the war with one hand tied behind their back. The USA had the military firepower to devastate North Vietnam and to cut off supplies to the north from China and the USSR. It was only late in the war that the USA began mining and bombing Haiphong harbour. Also, why didn't the USA and the ARVN simply invade and conquer North Vietnam? Johnson feared a repeat of the Korean War, where an invasion led to Chinese intervention. In 1966–70 China was experiencing political turmoil in the form of the Cultural Revolution. Johnson feared an invasion would escalate the conflict into a major Asian war, or possibly a nuclear confrontation with the USSR.

During the Korean War, US General Omar Bradley said that for the USA to expand the war into China would mean fighting 'the wrong war in the wrong place at the wrong time'. That view could equally have been applied to the USA's involvement in Vietnam. Its belief in the domino theory had drawn the USA into supporting a corrupt authoritarian regime under Diem until November 1963. Following Diem's assassination the South Vietnamese government suffered from chronic instability and corruption. In many ways the USA was drawn into a conflict it was unlikely ever to win. By the time the USA became fully involved, the cost of the war in terms of casualties and money proved to be too high a price to pay. US involvement cost the lives of 58,256 servicemen and the political careers of two presidents, Johnson and Nixon.

Since 1975 the USA has had to face the nightmare of Vietnam. A virtual industry has developed about the 'Nam experience'. Hollywood films such as *Apocalypse Now, The Deer Hunter, Platoon, Full Metal Jacket,* and *We Were Soldiers* tried to capture what it was like to fight. Other films such as *Taxi Driver, Coming Home* and *Born on the Fourth of July* showed what impact the war had on the subsequent lives of Vietnam veterans. In 1982 the Vietnam Veterans National Memorial was opened in Washington, DC. A black marble wall records the names of all the members of the US armed forces who died in Vietnam.

Questions
&
Answers

In this section there are two examination questions. They illustrate the range and type of source extracts and questions that you will come across.

Specimen answers are given for each examination question, one an A-grade and the other a C-grade response. All specimen answers are the subject of detailed examiner comments, preceded by the icon ⊘. You should study these comments carefully, because they show why and how marks are awarded and lost.

When examination papers are marked, all answers are given marks within levels of response. These levels are outlined in the introductory section of this guide.

Sub-question (a) is marked against three assessment objectives:
- Assessment objective AO1a tests the ability to recall, select and deploy relevant historical knowledge.
- Assessment objective AO1b tests the ability to understand the past through explanation and analysis and the ability to reach a judgement.
- Assessment objective AO2a tests the ability to engage in source analysis.

Sub-question (b) is marked against four assessment objectives:
- Assessment objective AO1a tests the ability to recall, select and deploy relevant historical knowledge.
- Assessment objective AO1b tests the ability to understand the past through explanation and analysis and the ability to reach a judgement.
- Assessment objective AO2a tests the ability to engage in source analysis.
- Assessment objective AO2b tests the ability to evaluate within historical context, showing how past events have been interpreted in different ways.

Question 1

Study the five sources on **US** involvement in the **Korean War** and answer both sub-questions.

(a) Study sources C and D.

Compare these sources as evidence of the reasons for **US** involvement in the **Korean War.**   (30 marks)

(b) Study all the sources.

Use your knowledge to assess how far the sources support the interpretation that the **US** commitment to defend South Korea was mainly to contain the spread of communism.   (70 marks)

Total: 100 marks

US involvement in the Korean War

Source A: *President Truman's statement about Korea, 26 June 1950*

The government of the United States is pleased with the speed and determination with which the United Nations Security Council acted to order a withdrawal of the invading forces...The United States will vigorously support the effort of the Council to terminate this serious breach of the peace...

Those responsible for this act of aggression must realise how seriously the government of the United States views such threats to the peace of the world.

Harry S. Truman Presidential Library

Source B: *UN Resolution on Korea, 27 June 1950*

The Security Council has determined that the armed attack on South Korea by forces from North Korea constitutes a breach of the peace. It also has called for an immediate cessation of hostilities. It has also noted an appeal from the Republic of Korea [South Korea] to the United Nations for immediate and effective steps to restore peace and security.

The Security Council recommends that the members of the United Nations furnish such assistance to South Korea as may be necessary to repel an armed attack and to restore international peace and security in the area.

Mount Holyoke College Library

question

Source C: *From a broadcast to the US people by President Truman, 27 June 1950*

The UN Security Council called on all members to render assistance to the United Nations. In these circumstances I have instructed the US air and sea forces to give South Korea support. The attack on Korea has made it clear beyond doubt that communism has passed beyond the use of subversion to conquer independent nations and will now use armed invasion and war. In these circumstances the occupation of Formosa [Nationalist China] by communist forces would be a direct threat to the security of the Pacific area and to United States forces operating there.

Accordingly, I have instructed the US 7th Fleet to prevent any attack on Formosa. I have directed that military assistance to the Philippines government be increased. I have similarly instructed military assistance to France in Indo-China to be accelerated.

Harry S. Truman Presidential Library

Source D: *Statement by the USSR Deputy Minister of Foreign Affairs, 4 July 1950*

What really happened? It is known that the United States government had started armed intervention in Korea before the Security Council was summoned to meet, without taking into consideration what decision the Security Council might take. The Security Council merely rubber-stamped and backdated the resolution proposed by the United States government, approving the aggressive actions which this government had undertaken.

If the Security Council valued the cause of peace, it should have attempted to reconcile the fighting sides in Korea before it adopted such a scandalous resolution.

Mount Holyoke College Library

Source E: *A modern historian considers the reasons for US involvement in the Korean War*

Kim's invasion — it was taken for granted that he had been sent south by Stalin — was the first real test for American resolve when confronted by Russian aggression. The domino theory was favoured. If Stalin were not stopped in Korea he would advance and states would fall in succession to communism until it dominated Europe and Asia or started a third world war. If Stalin went unchecked, US promises to resist communism in Europe and Asia would turn out to be hollow. The credibility of US foreign policy was at stake.

Martin McCauley, *Russia, America and the Cold War, 1949–1991*, 1998

A-grade answer to part (a)

(a) The decision by the USA to enter the Korean War has been the subject of some controversy. Literally within hours of receiving the news of the North Korean invasion of the south, US President Truman had ordered US troops to the Korean peninsula.

Source C is a broadcast to the American people which states the reasons why the USA became involved in the Korean War from the outset. Truman cites two main reasons for US involvement. Initially he states he is responding to the UN's request for support. This is found in the opening sentence, when Truman says: 'The UN Security Council called on all members to render assistance to the United Nations.' However, Truman goes on to state that a much broader reason for US involvement was to confront the expansion of communism in the far east. Clearly Truman believes in the 'domino theory', as he states that US military commitment is not merely limited to giving assistance to South Korea. It also involves supporting Nationalist China on Formosa, the Philippines and French Indo-China. Truman, in effect, is engaging in the containment of communism, an extension of his policies in Europe.

Source D, in contrast to source C, suggests that the UN merely backdated and rubber-stamped US military action, which had begun on the day of the North Korean invasion, 26 June. This contradicts Truman's claim that the USA acted in response to a UN request for assistance. It also suggests that US involvement was the result of its own aggression, not an attempt to resist North Korean aggression. However, it does support the view that the USA and UN acted together to resist the North Korean invasion because it suggests that the UN should have taken a different position by offering to mediate between the two sides.

President Truman's public announcement is useful because it was made the day after the invasion by North Korea and provided a clear justification of US actions. Truman had to justify to the American people why he was willing to send US troops into a war zone. However, the source is limited in the sense that it was a public announcement aimed at winning the support of the US public. As a result, he couched it in terms of an international Communist conspiracy affecting the whole of the far east. He states that Communist actions were part of a process which began with subversion, and if that did not work, would escalate into invasion and war to achieve their aim of expanding Communist control.

Source D is a statement by North Korea's ally, the USSR. With a global conflict between the USA and the USSR, the Deputy Minister of Foreign Affairs, one week after the US commitment to defend South Korea, attempts to justify North Korean action. He states that US action was deliberately belligerent and that the USA used the UN resolution as a smokescreen for aggression. His statement was made when both the USSR and North Korea were becoming increasingly isolated in the world community as other UN states supported UN and US military action to defend South Korea.

When we compare the two sources as evidence of the reasons for US involvement in the Korean War, source C is clearly a public attempt to justify US actions. In reality,

the US commitment to deploy troops predated the UN resolution on Korea. Source D, by a Soviet minister, like source C, is an attempted justification of why the war began. However, in this case the justification surrounds an attempt to defend the North Korean position by trying to blame the USA for aggression.

Therefore, the US decision to become involved in the Korean War was to support the UN but must also be seen in a broader perspective of trying to contain the expansion of communism in Asia.

The answer offers a clear and concise focus on the question. It is structured logically, dealing with areas of comparison and contrast between the two sources. Where appropriate, historical terminology is used, such as the reference to the containment of communism. Also, where appropriate, relevant quotations from the sources are used to support and sustain an argument.

The structure of the answer is analytical. It provides a relevant introduction and makes a clear comparison, which where appropriate is placed in historical context.

Clear reference is made to the provenance of both sources. Mention is made of the author, date, audience and motive behind each source.

Finally, the answer reaches a clear judgement in the final paragraph.

Using the mark scheme, this answer was awarded Level 1A, with 5 marks for AO1a, 8 marks for AO1b and 15 marks for AO2a.

Total: 28/30 marks

■ ■ ■

C-grade answer to part (a)

(a) The two sources, C and D, offer a valuable insight into why the USA became involved in the Korean War.

Source C clearly states that the USA entered the conflict in support of the United Nations. The US president, Harry S. Truman, makes it clear that the USA abhors North Korean aggression and this is the reason why he was willing to commit US troops to the conflict. To Truman the Communists in the north had gone beyond trying to subvert the government of South Korea and had engaged in invasion and an attempted conquest of the South. The source suggests strongly that the USA was reacting in response to North Korean aggression.

Source D takes a very different point of view. It is produced by the Soviet Deputy Minister of Foreign Affairs and will therefore offer a Communist perspective on the start of the conflict. Instead of being reactive the USA is portrayed as an aggressor. To this author the USA is working with the UN but he sees the relationship the other way around. He states that the UN merely rubber-stamped the US decision to intervene militarily. He suggests that the UN's time would be better used trying to get a negotiated settlement.

Therefore, both sources support the view that the USA worked closely with the UN in supporting South Korea in its attempt to halt a North Korean invasion. The two sources differ in the sense that in source C the USA responded to a UN call for action, while source D suggests that the UN merely rubber-stamped US military action already ordered by President Truman.

✍ **The answer is relevant throughout. It is structured and generally coherent, with a good attempt at both explanation and analysis. Reference is made to information from both sources. The answer contrasts the suggestions that the USA was reactive in source C, and proactive in source D, in terms of taking military action. There is a clear understanding of the relationship between the USA and the UN, although it would have been useful to mention that the USA was a member of the main decision-making body, the UN Security Council.**

There is a relevant comparison and contrast between the two sources. However, the references to the provenance of both sources could have been more comprehensive. The answer doesn't mention the timing and audience of either source.

Finally the answer doesn't deal with important aspects of source C, such as Truman's reference to defending other non-Communist Asian countries, which had an important bearing on the motives for US involvement.

Using the marking grid, this answer was awarded an overall grade Level II, with 4 marks for AO1a, 5 marks for AO1b and 11 marks for AO2a.

Total: 20/30 marks

■ ■ ■

A-grade answer to part (b)

(b) Between 1950 and 1953 the USA fought its first major war since 1945 in an attempt to defend South Korea against a North Korean invasion which was an attempt to unite the Korean peninsula. At the time of the invasion the USA claimed it was acting in response to a request by the United Nations. However, was the USA's real intent to contain the spread of communism?

To a degree, information in the sources suggests that the USA wished to contain communism. This is stated most clearly in sources C and E. Source C, a public broadcast by President Truman to the American people, made the day after the North Korean invasion, makes it clear that the USA wished to contain communism. It makes clear that US military commitments in Asia are not to be limited merely to defending South Korea. US military commitment was extended to other areas which Truman believed were subject to Communist aggression. These included Nationalist China.

Since the end of the Chinese Civil War in 1949, and the proclamation of the People's Republic of China, there was a belief that Communist China might invade the last remaining part of China under Nationalist control, the island of Formosa (modern-day Taiwan). Also, source C states that the USA will support the French in their conflict with the Communist Vietminh in Indo-China.

This view is supported by source E, which states clearly that the USA supported the domino theory. The source states that the whole of US foreign policy credibility was at stake. If Truman did not take a stand against communism in Korea, then the US policy of containment of communism in both Europe and Asia would be under threat. In 1949 the USA had helped to create NATO to contain Communist expansion in Europe. Now the Cold War had been extended to Asia. To Truman and his advisors, this was part of the same process.

As the war progressed, Truman and his military commander in Korea, General Douglas MacArthur, continually spoke of the conflict in terms of communism versus the Free World. In October 1950, UN forces under US command decided to go beyond the UN resolution of 27 June and invaded North Korea. In this sense, US involvement in the Korean War went beyond containing communism and, instead, attempted to roll back communism from the Korean peninsula.

However, it could be argued that the USA merely acted on behalf of the UN. Source A supports this view. The statement was made on the day of the North Korean invasion and makes it clear that the USA is acting on behalf of the UN. This view is supported in source C, made the following day, when Truman repeats the US commitment to support the UN request for support for South Korea. Truman realised that if the UN was to be an effective international organisation in defence of peace and international security it had to act decisively. The UN resolution, source B, supports the view that the UN attempted to act decisively. UN action transcended US attempts to contain communism because the UN request was answered by a wide variety of countries such as the UK, Turkey, Greece, Italy and France. As a result, the US decision to be engaged in the Korean War had a strong UN element. This is supported by the fact that the USA referred to its involvement in the Korean War as a police action in support of the UN.

This position can also be defended through reference to Dean Acheson's 'Defense Perimeter' speech at the beginning of 1950. Acheson, the US Secretary of State, referred to US attempts to contain communism in Asia through the announcement of a defence perimeter. The Korean peninsula was not mentioned, which suggests that it was outside the area where the USA planned to contain communism.

However, source D suggests strongly that US concerns about communism and its expansion were the main factor behind US involvement. The source suggests that the UN was used merely as a smokescreen to cover US attempts to contain communism. In one sense, the author of the source, a leading Soviet minister, was attempting to defend North Korea, a fellow Communist state, however it does contain an element of truth. The US decision to intervene predated the UN resolution on Korea. In this sense the UN merely 'rubber-stamped' US military assistance to South Korea.

There is strong evidence to suggest that the USA acted in defence of the UN. This is made clear in sources A, B and C. However, throughout the conflict US policy-makers referred to the conflict as an attempt to limit the growth of communism. This position is supported in sources C, D and E. The fact that the USA began to refer to the Bamboo Curtain in Asia as an equivalent of the Iron Curtain in Europe supports this position.

On balance, it would seem that the USA became involved in the Korean War to contain the expansion of communism. The actions by Truman mentioned in source C suggest a wider US commitment to defend Asian states against communism. This position is supported by the fact that in the wake of the Korean War, the USA was the driving force behind the military alliances SEATO and CENTO, part of a worldwide attempt to contain communism.

🖉 **This is a focused answer. The introduction is relevant and provides a clear introduction to the analysis that follows. The answer refers to all five sources and integrates relevant own knowledge with source material to develop a clear, logical and consistent analysis.**

The answer reaches a clear judgement in the conclusion which deals directly with the interpretation in the question.

Using the marking grid, this answer was awarded 9 marks under AO1a, 11 marks under AO1b, 27 marks under AO2a and 20 marks under AO2b, all in Level IA.

Total: 67/70 marks

■ ■ ■

C-grade answer to part (b)

(b) The decision by the USA to become involved militarily in the Korean War helped globalise the Cold War. Until 1950 the conflict had largely been confined to Europe. However, as a result of US involvement the Cold War was extended to Asia.

The view that the USA was now fighting a Cold War in Asia is supported by a number of sources. Source C states that the USA is not only going to help South Korea, but also other Asian countries fighting communism. These include Formosa, the Philippines and the French in Indo-China. From 1950 the USA began by deploying more of its armed forces in Asia. Japan became a major US military base: in particular, the island of Okinawa. The USA also signed defence agreements with Japan, Formosa, the Philippines and, after 1954, with non-Communist governments in southeast Asia.

The anti-Communist nature of US involvement is also suggested in source E, which gives a longer-term view of US involvement, being written in 1991. It suggests that Truman believed in the domino theory and he had to confront communism in South Korea. Even source D, written by a Soviet minister, suggests that US actions were anti-Communist in intent.

However, sources A and B suggest a different motive for US action. Both sources state that the USA, as a member of the UN, is reacting to a call by the UN Security Council to stand up to North Korean aggression. Both the US president, on the day of the invasion, and the UN resolution shortly afterwards state clearly that they are merely resisting aggression against a neutral country.

Therefore, the weight of evidence from the sources, and my own knowledge, suggests strongly that the USA became involved in the Korean War mainly to resist the expansion of Communist control in Asia.

> **The answer is clearly focused on the question. All five sources are used to develop a balanced analytical answer. The information provided is accurate but the use of own knowledge is limited. The answer depends heavily on information from the sources. The correct historical terminology is used and there is a good attempt at explanation and analysis.**
>
> **Using the marking grid, the answer was awarded 7 marks under AO1a, 7 marks under AO1b, 20 marks under AO2a and 14 marks under AO2b, with an overall result of low Level II.**

Total: 48/70 marks

Question 2

Study the five sources on the Tet Offensive of 1968 and then answer both sub-questions.

(a) Study sources B and E.

Compare these sources as evidence of the impact of the Tet Offensive on US involvement in South Vietnam. (30 marks)

(b) Study all the sources.

Use your knowledge to assess how far the sources support the interpretation that the Tet Offensive was not a failure for the USA. (70 marks)

Total: 100 marks

Source A: *Press briefing by US General Westmoreland, Commander-in-chief in Vietnam, 16 November 1967.*

REPORTER: How do you see it, General?

GENERAL WESTMORELAND: Very very encouraged. I've never been more encouraged during my entire, almost 4 years in this country. I think we're making real progress. Everybody is very optimistic that I know of, who is intimately associated with our effort there.

Vietnam: A Television History, PBS, 1981

Source B: *Leading US newscaster Walter Cronkite's view of the Tet Offensive, 27 February 1968.*

We'd like to sum up our findings in Vietnam, an analysis that must be speculative, personal, and subjective. Who won and who lost in the great Tet Offensive against the cities? I'm not sure. The Vietcong did not win by a knockout, but neither did we. The referees of history may make it a draw. Another standoff may be coming in the big battles expected south of the DMZ. Khe Sanh could well fall, with a terrible loss in American lives, prestige and morale...On the political front, past performance gives no confidence that the Vietnamese government can cope with its problems, now compounded by the attack on the cities.

Reporting Vietnam: Part One: American Journalism 1959–1969, 1998

question

Source C: *US Secretary of State in 1968, Dean Rusk, remembers his views of the Tet Offensive, 1981.*

Even though it was a considerable military set-back for the North Vietnamese and Vietcong out there on the ground, it was, in effect, a brilliant political victory for them here in the United States. I'm not sure I fully understand the reasons why that should have occurred, but it became very clear after the Tet Offensive that many people at the grass roots, such as my cousins in Cherokee County, finally came to the conclusion that if we could not tell them when this war was going to end, and we couldn't in any good faith, that we might as well chuck it.

Vietnam: A Television History, PBS, 1981

Source D: *Tran Van Tra, a Vietcong member during the Tet Offensive, recollects, 1982.*

During Tet of 1968 we did not correctly evaluate the specific balance of forces between ourselves and the enemy, did not fully realise that the enemy still had considerable capabilities and that our capabilities were limited. Although that decision was wise and timely, and its implementation was well organised and bold, there was excellent coordination on all battlefields, everyone acted bravely, sacrificed their lives, and there was created a significant strategic turning point in Vietnam, we suffered large sacrifices and losses with regard to manpower and materiel which clearly weakened us.

Tran Van Tra, *Vietnam, Vol. 5: Concluding the 30-Years War*, 1982

Source E: *US journalist James Willbanks appraises the Tet Offensive, 29 January 2009.*

This week, we mark the 41st anniversary of the 1968 Tet Offensive, generally recognised as the watershed event of the US war in Vietnam. The outcome of the offensive ultimately led to a major shift in American strategy from trying to defeat the Vietcong and North Vietnamese Army to finding a way to disengage from the conflict. That being said, it is easy 41 years later to forget that the Tet Offensive was a crushing defeat for the Communist forces. It was simply the audacity and ferocity of the attack that caught American leaders so off guard and so shocked American TV viewers that the course of the war changed in an instant, ending the presidency of Lyndon Baines Johnson in the process.

James Willbanks, *US News*, January 2009

■ ■ ■

A-grade answer to part (a)

(a) The Tet Offensive of early 1968 was one of the most important episodes in the USA's involvement in the Vietnam War and these two sources provide different perspectives on its impact.

Source B is by a leading US news broadcaster who is reporting his own personal views of the Tet Offensive, at the height of the offensive in February 1968. He claims that the conflict in Vietnam is a stalemate rather than a US defeat. Yet he does state that if Khe Sanh fell during the offensive it could undermine the whole US military position in Vietnam.

Cronkite regards the most important impact of the Tet Offensive as its role in undermining the government of South Vietnam. Cronkite states: 'On the political front, past performance gives no confidence that the Vietnamese government can cope with its problems, now compounded by the attack on the cities.' To Cronkite, the Tet Offensive seems to be the last straw in his negative appraisal of South Vietnam, the country US troops are trying to protect and defend. Therefore, the Tet Offensive had a major negative impact on US involvement in Vietnam.

The other source, source E, also suggests the Tet Offensive had a negative impact on US involvement. Written over 40 years after the events, it offers a broader, more contextual view of its impact. The journalist states that the Tet Offensive resulted in a major shift in US policy from trying to defeat the Communists to trying to achieve a negotiated peace.

However, James Willbanks, in source E, sees the impact of the Tet Offensive from a different perspective to source B. Rather than concentrating on the impact of the offensive on the government of South Vietnam, he refers directly to the offensive's impact on the USA and its policy. He states that images of the offensive changed US public opinion dramatically. It even resulted in the decision by President Johnson not to stand for re-election to the presidency.

Source E offers a more useful assessment. It is not a personal view made at the time but a more measured view made in hindsight some 40 years after the event. It also deals directly with the impact on US public opinion and on the presidency.

As a result, both sources state that the Tet Offensive had a significant impact on the USA, both in undermining the South Vietnamese government and in changing US public opinion.

This answer is clearly focused on the question throughout. The introduction, although short, is concise and sets out the parameters for future explanation and analysis.

The use of historical terminology is accurate throughout and the paragraphs are structured clearly and logically.

2

question

The answer deals with both comparisons and areas of contrast between the two sources which are linked directly to the question asked. The sources have been quoted appropriately.

The answer also makes direct and relevant use of the provenance of both sources in terms of their reliability, utility and consistency.

The answer reaches a valid judgement in the final paragraph.

Using the marking grid, the answer was awarded **6 marks under AO1a**, **7 marks under AO1b** and **16 marks in AO2a**, which gave it an overall result of **Level IA.**

Total: 29/30 marks

■ ■ ■

C-grade answer to part (a)

(a) Both the sources suggest that the Tet Offensive had a big impact on US involvement in Vietnam.

Source B is by a US television news broadcaster. He suggests that the Tet Offensive is likely to end in stalemate. He states that he thought, before the Tet Offensive, that the USA was winning the war. Now he feels he is not so sure. He even goes as far to state that the fall of Khe Sanh may well undermine the US effort in South Vietnam. His main conclusion refers to the US ally South Vietnam. He believes that the attack on the cities undermines the authority of the government of South Vietnam and, no doubt, US involvement in Vietnam.

Source E also offers a similar view. It states that the images of the Tet Offensive shown in America shocked the US public and undermined their confidence in winning the war. It brought about a major change in opinion. From the Tet Offensive onwards the USA was looking for a negotiated peace rather than outright military victory over the Communists. It is significant that both sources have a similar view even though one, source B, is a primary source, written at the time of the Tet Offensive and the other, source E, was written 41 years after the event.

Therefore, the Tet Offensive had a major impact on the US involvement because it helped bring about a major change in US public opinion and helped undermine the presidency of Lyndon Johnson.

✐ The answer is relevant and both compares and contrasts the information contained within both sources. The introduction is rather short and offers only general coverage of the subject to be discussed.

The answer uses relevant information from within both sources to make a clear and logical case.

However, reference to the provenance of both sources is limited throughout and there is only a partial reference to the reliability, utility and completeness of explanation contained within the sources.

Using the marking grid, this answer was awarded 5 marks under AO1a, 5 marks under AO1b and 11 marks under AO2a, giving an overall result on the border between Level II and Level III.

Total: 21/30 marks

■ ■ ■

A-grade answer to part (b)

b) The Tet Offensive was one of the most defining moments in the US involvement in the Vietnam War. The offensive shocked US public opinion and helped change fundamentally US perceptions of the war.

Tet undermined Johnson's presidency and helped fuel the anti-war movement within the USA. However, was the Tet Offensive a complete failure for the USA?

Source D is an assessment of the Tet Offensive from a Communist point of view. Although produced 14 years after the event it is the view of a member of the Vietcong who participated in the Tet Offensive. It states clearly, from a military viewpoint, that the offensive was not a total success for the Communists. In contrast, it states that the Communists underestimated US military strength and resolve, with the effect that the Tet Offensive led to the Communists suffering 'large sacrifices and losses with regard to manpower and materiel which clearly weakened us'.

This view is supported by source E, which states 41 years after the event that the offensive was a 'crushing defeat for the Communists'. In fact, the Tet Offensive destroyed the military capabilities of the National Liberation Front. Increasingly after Tet the main thrust of the Communist military activity campaign came from the North Vietnamese Army. Dean Rusk, the US Secretary of State in 1968, also states that the offensive was a major military setback for the Communists.

However, the impact of the Tet Offensive cannot be judged only in military terms. It is true that the NLF lost thousands of front-line guerrilla fighters and the marine base at Khe Sanh was relieved. However, the political impact of the offensive, in retrospect, was far greater. Part of the problem was the surprise and astonishment felt by many Americans at the time. Source A suggests that this element of surprise was also felt by the US military command in Vietnam. In Source A , as late as 16 December 1967, General Westmoreland was telling the US press that the US military was making real progress and he was very optimistic about the future. The Tet Offensive and the siege of Khe Sanh changed all this. The sight of Vietcong guerrillas within the US embassy compound in Saigon amazed many Americans watching events unfold on their televisions. Westmoreland's optimistic views stood in stark contrast to the sight of Communists actually on US soil.

2

question

This view is supported by both sources B and C. Walter Cronkite, the most influential television news broadcaster, visited South Vietnam shortly after the outbreak of the offensive. He reported his personal views at the end of February. He suggested that the USA was not winning in Vietnam and was facing a stalemate. To him, after a long series of over-optimistic reports from the US government and military, it seemed that the time had come for the USA to consider withdrawal. President Johnson stated, after watching Cronkite's news broadcast: 'If I have lost Walter, I have lost Mr Average Citizen.'

The idea that US public opinion altered dramatically as a result of the Tet Offensive is also mentioned in source C. Former US Secretary of State Dean Rusk stated in 198 that the offensive had a marked effect on his own family and their view of the war. He states that their view changed to one of supporting US withdrawal. Even source D by a Vietcong guerrilla, states that although the Communists suffered heavy losses the Tet Offensive was a 'strategic turning point' in the Vietnam War.

Source E, which offers a long-term perspective, regards the offensive as a watershed in US involvement, resulting in a major shift in US policy. Out went the idea that the Communists could be defeated, to be replaced by a new policy of trying to get a negotiated settlement. Source E also reinforces the view that the offensive had a profound effect on US public opinion. It states that the ferocity of the Communist attacks shocked the US public as they watched scenes from the Tet Offensive almost nightly on their television sets.

Perhaps the height of failure for the Americans came when, on 31 March 1968 President Johnson announced his decision not to stand for re-election.

Therefore, on one hand the Tet Offensive was a military victory for the USA. Thousands of Vietcong guerrillas had been killed. However, the offensive helped destroy the credibility of the US military command, which had been so optimistic in its assessment of the war. The offensive also shocked and changed US public opinion in a profound way and made the Tet Offensive a turning point in US involvement in the war.

> **The answer uses a wide range of relevant evidence organised into a clearly structured logical argument which reaches a judgement.**
>
> **The introduction is relevant and offers a clear link to subsequent explanation.**
>
> **All five sources are used and the evidence from these sources is applied relevantly throughout. Where appropriate, relevant quotations from the sources are used to support and sustain a clear argument.**
>
> **Source material and own knowledge are integrated to produce a balanced analysis required by the question.**
>
> **The interpretation cited in the question is referred to throughout the answer, and the conclusion flows logically from the argument presented.**

Using the marking grid, this answer was awarded **9** marks under **AO1a**, **11** marks under **AO1b**, **26** marks under **AO2a** and **20** marks under **AO2b**, all within Level IA.

Total: 66/70 marks

■ ■ ■

C-grade answer to part (b)

(b) The Tet Offensive can be regarded as a major turning point in US involvement in Vietnam. Before that date the USA thought it could win the war. After Tet the USA began thinking about a way out through a negotiated settlement.

The difference between before and after the Tet Offensive can be seen in sources A and C. Source A, written before the offensive, suggests that the USA is winning the war. General Westmoreland, the US commander of MACV, states clearly that the USA is very optimistic about winning the war. However, in source C, by Dean Rusk, US Secretary of State in 1968, the scenes of the Tet Offensive undermined US support for the war. Rusk states that his relations began thinking that the USA would be better withdrawing.

The idea that the Tet Offensive was a failure is also mentioned in source E, which was written 41 years after the event. It states that Tet was a watershed in US involvement in Vietnam, leading to a major shift in US policy towards a negotiated peace. The Vietcong guerrilla in 1968, the author of source D, also states that the offensive was a strategic victory for the Communists.

Clearly the Tet Offensive was a major turning point. It led to more anti-war demonstrations within the USA and even led President Johnson to end his bid for re-election.

Yet there is evidence to suggest that the Tet Offensive was not a failure for the USA. Source B, by Walter Cronkite, talks of a stalemate, not a defeat. Dean Rusk, in source C, states that the offensive was a severe military setback for the Communists, a view shared by source E. Even source D, which is a Communist source by someone who fought in the Tet Offensive, stated that it had caused considerable Communist casualties and the impact of Tet was to weaken the Communist side.

Therefore, the Tet Offensive was a failure for the USA in a political sense. It undermined the South Vietnamese government and helped change US public opinion and US policy in Vietnam. Yet from a military point of view, it could be said that it was not a failure. US and ARVN forces inflicted a major military setback on the Communists, but on balance the political effects were more important.

🖉 **The answer is focused on the question. All five sources are used, but the material taken from the sources is limited and lacking detail.**

The use of own knowledge, although present, is also limited in range and depth.

An attempt has been made to refer to the provenance of the sources but this is also limited.

However, the answer does offer a balanced explanation which is linked directly to the interpretation in the question.

A conclusion is included which reaches a judgement in a limited way.

Using the marking grid, this answer was awarded 6 marks under AO1a, 7 marks under AO1b, 19 marks under AO2a and 12 marks under AO2b, with an overall result of Level III.

Total: 44/70 marks

PHILIP ALLAN
UPDATES

Intensive Revision Weekends

Biology

Business Studies (AQA)

Chemistry

Economics

French

German

Law (AQA or OCR)

Mathematics

Physics (Edexcel)

Politics

Psychology (AQA (A))

Religious Studies

Sociology

Spanish

- Intensive 2-day revision courses with expert tutors, including senior examiners
- Guaranteed to improve exam technique and build confidence
- Develops AS and A2 key skills
- Tests understanding of core topics
- Invaluable summary notes provided
- Ideal Central London location

Contact us today for further information: tel: 01706 831002 fax: 01706 830011
e-mail: sales@philipallanupdates.co.uk

Philip Allan Updates
Suite 16, Hardmans Business Centre, Rossendale, Lancashire BB4 6HH